3-23-60

THE BIBLE AND RACE

The **BIBLE**
and **RACE**

T. B. Maston

BROADMAN PRESS
Nashville, Tennessee

© 1959 · BROADMAN PRESS
Nashville, Tennessee

All rights reserved
International copyright secured

422–07174

Library of Congress catalog card number: 59–5858

Printed in the United States of America

5.AT58K.S.P.

1111998

To
Some Courageous Friends
Who Are Maintaining
Bridges of Understanding
in
Times of Tension

PREFACE

There was a sense of increasing acuteness concerning the race issue in the world in general and in the United States in particular even before the Supreme Court school desegregation decision of May 17, 1954. The feeling of urgency was heightened tremendously, however, when the Court made its decision.

The Bible has been drawn in various ways into the subsequent controversy. While the Bible has very little to say directly on race, it does contain some basic concepts that are relevant to the problem. The present volume is an attempt to state and to interpret some of these concepts. The exposition of the Scriptures is the main emphasis. There is no attempt to study in general the various aspects of the race problem. For a person to receive the maximum benefit from a study of these chapters he should have a Bible readily available.

Possibly a word should be said about the relation of this book to an earlier volume, entitled *Of One,* which was written approximately ten years ago for the Home Mission Board of the Southern Baptist Convention. That book was prepared as a study guide on the race problem, for use primarily by church women. It has been out of print for some time. The present volume replaces *Of One.* It is not a revision of the latter. It is true that some of the chapter headings are retained and limited portions of the material incorporated. However, there are three or four entirely new chapters, and most of the material in the other chapters is decidedly different from the earlier book.

Gratitude is expressed to a number of busy people who

PREFACE

have taken the time to read the manuscript—Guy Bellamy,
John Caylor, Joe Green, Mrs. William D. McMurry, and
three of my fellow teachers, C. W. Scudder, William Rossell,
and Ray Summers. The last two gave particular attention to
the interpretation of the Scriptures. Each of those who read
the manuscript made distinctive and constructive contribu-
tions to its improvement. Needless to say, however, they are
not responsible in any way for what is said in the book. That
is my responsibility alone.

I am indebted to the typists who have assisted at various
stages with the manuscript—Miss Betty Francis and Mrs.
Melvin B. Bridgford.

Several translations of the Bible are used. Where the
version is not indicated, the quotation is *from the Revised
Standard Version of the Bible.* Copyrighted 1946 and 1952.

T. B. MASTON

CONTENTS

CONTENTS

Love and the Law
The Language of Love

I

"IN THE IMAGE OF GOD"

*So God created man in his own image, in the
image of God created he him; male and female
created he them.*　　　　GENESIS 1:27, AV

There is abundant evidence that man was the
crowning act of God's creative work. Even on the surface of
the creation story there is a difference in the approach to the
creation of man. Notice that the first day the record simply
says, "And God said, Let there be light: and there was light"
(Gen. 1:3, AV). But for the creation of man it says, "And
God said, Let us make man in our image, after our likeness"
(Gen. 1:26, AV). "The language is suggestive of pause and
deliberation." [1] Whether the "us" refers to God as Father,
Son,[2] and Holy Spirit or means that God was communicat-
ing with angels or celestial beings or simply that he was talking to himself, certainly there is considerable dignity and suggested significance in the approach to the task.

The threefold use of the word "created" in verse 27 also
adds some weight and importance to the occasion. It is a
threefold parallelism, a "kind of solemn chant," "a song of
jubilation over the creation of man." [3] From every point of
view man is seen to be the climax of God's creation. One evidence of this fact was the dominion that God gave him over
the rest of creation. He was created to dominate, not to be

[1] Calvin Goodspeed and D. M. Welton, *The Book of Genesis* in *An
American Commentary on the Old Testament* (Philadelphia: American
Baptist Publication Society, 1908), p. 50.
[2] The following are some New Testament references to the part Christ
played in the creation of the world: John 1:3; 1 Cor. 8:6; Col. 1:16; and
Heb. 1:2.
[3] Goodspeed and Welton, *op. cit.*, p. 51.

dominated. Domination by his fellow man means pulling him down to the animal level.

The psalmist asked a searching question and then gave a hint at an answer when he said:

> What is man that thou art mindful of him,
>   and the son of man that thou dost care for him?
> Yet thou hast made him little less than God,
>   and dost crown him with glory and honor.
> Thou hast given him dominion over the works of thy hands,
>   thou hast put all things under his feet. (Psalm 8:4-6).

God has given man dominion over that which God himself has created. In a sense he is God's representative. God has delegated some of his power to the one he has created in his own image. The dominion is the consequence or result of the image, although it was not and is not the content of the image.[4]

That man is closely related to the animal world is implied by the fact that he was created on the same day that God said, "Let the earth bring forth living creatures according to their kinds: cattle and creeping things and beasts of the earth according to their kinds" (Gen. 1:24). On the other hand, the distinctive nature of man's creation is revealed by the transition from "let the earth bring forth" to "let us make man." Here is something unique and different. Man, created in the image of God, is at least the "king and crown" of all animal creation, having authority over it.

While there is a sense in which man belongs to, and may be identified with, nature, there is another very true and deep sense in which he transcends nature. It is the image of God within which enables him to transcend nature and even, in a sense, to transcend or stand outside of himself. So far as we know, man is the only one of God's created beings that can look himself in the face and more or less objectively ex-

---

[4] Franz Delitzsch, *A New Commentary on Genesis*, trans. Sophia Taylor (New York: Scribner and Welford, 1889), I, 100.

amine and analyze himself. Let us not forget, however, that the thing that makes him most distinctly man is his capacity for fellowship or communion with God. This capacity is given to men of all classes and races. There is no partiality with God. It is man, representative of all men, who is created in the image of God. The image is not restricted to red or yellow, black or white.

Interpretation of the Image

What does it mean for man to be created in the image of God? The interpretation of the expression has real significance in the whole area of race relations. Christian students and scholars have differed and do differ considerably in their interpretation of the image.

One viewpoint concerning the image, which gets close to the root of the matter, is that God is a person and that man is like God in that he also is a person. But what does it mean to be a person? Personality involves, in addition to the power to reason, at least two other qualities: self-consciousness and a sense of moral responsibility. There is no self-consciousness without the consciousness of others. The two go together and progress together. There is a sense, however, in which the individual tends to lose consciousness of the self as he becomes increasingly conscious of others and particularly of his responsibilities for others. Somewhat paradoxically, this forgetfulness of the self leads to the highest fulfilment of the self. The fact that we find life by losing it is a fundamental law of life.

The sense of moral responsibility is closely related to the development of the self. Maturing individuals, maturing Christians in particular, have a growing sense of responsibility for and to other persons. The highest level of moral development is reached only when this sense of responsibility is related to the supreme Person and to his demands upon, and expectations of, us. However, the highest levels of ethical living are not reached by the Christian until his devotion to

3

God and to the service of his fellow man is a natural result of his own inner desires rather than a result of a sense of obligation, of a premeditated, calculating obedience to the demands of the moral law.

Pieters sums up the meaning of the image as follows: "Any being that can say to himself: 'I am, I ought, I will,' is made in the image of God." [5] This statement includes most of what we have suggested so far. The "I am" can be equated with self-consciousness, the "I ought" with the sense of moral accountability, and the "I will" with the power of self-determination, which is essential for moral responsibility.

There is, however, at least one other element in the image-of-God concept which needs to be emphasized. James Orr, in defining the image, touches on this element. He not only stresses the self-consciousness of the human person and the sense and power of moral responsibility, but he adds the "capacity for fellowship with God." [6] This capacity for fellowship is particularly important and possibly comes closest to an adequate definition of the meaning of "the image of God." Personality, both on the human and the divine levels, involves and necessitates fellowship, or communication. This means that anything that artificially limits or destroys one's fellowship with his fellow man will impoverish his personality.

This idea of communication is implied in the creation of man and woman. Notice that the record says, "In the image of God created he him; male and female created he them." Later, in giving "the book of the generations of Adam," reference is made to the original creation and to the creation of male and female (Gen. 5:1–2). The other specific reference in the Old Testament to the image of God in man implies the creation of male and female (Gen. 9:5–7).

[5] Albertus Pieters, *Notes on Genesis* (2d ed.; Grand Rapids: Wm. B. Eerdmans Publishing Co., 1947), p. 47.
[6] James Orr, *God's Image in Man* (London: Hodder & Stoughton, 1905), p. 57.

It is plainly stated in Genesis 2:18 that God said, "It is not good that the man should be alone; I will make him a help meet for him" (ASV). The marginal reading in the American Standard Version says "answering to him." God says, "I will make him one answering to him." Woman answers to man in the same sense that he answers to her. They supplement one another, they find their fulfilment in one another. They are created to answer to one another like the violin and bow are made to find their fulfilment in one another.

In a broader sense, men as such are made to answer to one another. They are made to communicate with one another. The individual becomes a person through such communication. It is not good for men to dwell alone. It is no accident that Robinson Crusoe was a purely fictitious character, and even he had his man Friday.

Man alone of God's created beings has the capacity for an I-thou relation, not only with man but also with God. It is man's capacity for communion with God that makes him most distinctly a being created in the image of God. He has the power to respond to God's self-disclosure or self-communication. He must respond if there is to be any real communion. God's revelation or communication of himself is a transitive event. He may be and is the initiator of the revelation. He is the subject, but there must also be a recipient or an object of the revelation. In other words, God is limited by our willingness to listen and to have communion with him.

Man not only has the capacity and the responsibility to respond to God; he is also restless and has a sense of homelessness until he does respond. The image of God within man finds its fulfilment in fellowship with his Creator, who is the source of the image and the perfect embodiment of that which is very imperfectly expressed even in the most mature child of God. It was Augustine who said, "Thou madest us for Thyself, and our heart is restless, until it repose in Thee." [7]

[7] *The Confessions of Saint Augustine* (New York: The Modern Library, 1949), p. 3.

5

This restlessness—which is particularly acute before conversion, but which continues even after conversion as an expression of our imperfection—helps to explain the continuous, never-ending search by man for God and for a better understanding of God's ways in the world.

Sin and the Image

Man, who was created in the image of God, was tempted and sinned, and in a sense he was re-created in the image of sin. Sin became an integral part of the heritage of the human race. "Sin came into the world through one man [Adam] and death through sin" (Rom. 5:12). Sin, however, became not only a part of man's inheritance; it also became a very real personal experience in his life. "All we like sheep have gone astray" (Isa. 53:6). "None is righteous, no, not one" (Rom. 3:10). Jew and Gentile alike are included. "No one does good, not even one" (Rom. 3:12).

This is true of the so-called saint and sinner, of those of every nationality, class, or race. All are under condemnation for sin. The wages of sin is death, and death means separation—separation from God and hope. Not only are all under condemnation for sin but the same provision for release from the penalty and power or enslavement of sin has been made for all. While the wages of sin is death, yet "the free gift of God is eternal life in Christ Jesus our Lord" (Rom. 6:23). While we all like sheep have gone astray, yet "the Lord has laid on him [Christ] the iniquity of us all" (Isa. 53:6).

What has sin done to the image of God in man? Has sin destroyed that image, marred or defaced it or left it largely, if not entirely, untouched? The answer to those questions is of considerable importance for human relations. If respect for human personality is based and dependent upon the fact that man was created in the image of God—and it is—then if that image was completely destroyed in man or in any segment of mankind, there would not be left any valid basis for universal respect for men. The only ones with real worth and

6

dignity would be those who had had the image restored through the operation of divine grace.

There seem to be some persons who believe and act as if the image of God in man, at least in some men, has been completely destroyed. Such a position, however, is not in harmony with the revelation that we have from God. For example, long after sin had entered the human race and even after the terrible sins preceding the Flood, God revealed to Noah that murder was wrong and was to be punished, because man was created in the image of God (Gen. 9:6). This suggests that at least enough of the image was left to make man sacred in the sight of God. If he is sacred in the sight of God, he should be sacred in the eyes of God's children.

What if the image were totally destroyed and could not be restored except through faith in Christ, an experience which makes the person a new creation in Christ Jesus? Is such a saving faith limited to any class or racial group? The "whosoevers" of the gospel sufficiently answer the question. Even if the only ones who are of infinite worth and dignity are those in whom the image has been restored, yet they come from north and south, east and west. In Christ there is neither male nor female, bond nor free, Jew nor Gentile, red nor yellow, black nor white. They are all precious in his sight. How grateful we ought to be for that fact! If God were a respecter of persons, some of us would not have been included in the provisions of his marvelous grace.

We have stated that the main emphasis in the image is that man is a person, that he is made for communion, or communication, with God and his fellow human beings. While sin has marred this capacity for communication, both on the social and on the spiritual levels, it has not totally destroyed it. We should remember, however, that sin separates. It was sin that drove Adam and Eve from the garden and from the presence of God. Sin either separates from God or God separates us from sin. Sin also separates us from our fellow men. However, while man in his sinful state may not be able to communicate with God, yet he retains the potentiality. Regardless of what has happened to him, he was created for such communion and does not lose that potentiality because of his sin. He retains the capacity to approach or to recede from the likeness of God. "The resemblance can never be perfect: but it can increase and it can diminish." [8]

There is almost universal agreement among biblical scholars, past and present, that the image of God was not totally destroyed when man sinned. They generally agree that there is at least enough of the image left to be a point of contact within man for God and to make man responsible to God. The image as a point of contact for God is one of the main hopes of the one who proclaims the message of Christ. There is enough of the image left to say yes to the gospel when it is proclaimed to the man in sin.

The idea of the responsibility of man as a phase of the image of God in all men may be implied by what Paul says in the first two chapters of Romans. He says that all men are without excuse (Rom. 1:20). Even the Gentiles, who have not the law, have a law written in their hearts (Rom. 2:14–15). Could this law, this innate sense of oughtness, be an evidence and an expression of the image of God within man, which has been marred but not totally destroyed?

Restoration of the Image

In the Old Testament the emphasis is on the universal image, which is common to all men. In the New Testament the emphasis is primarily on the restoration of the image of God in man through faith in the living Christ.

The New Testament reveals that Christ is the image, or likeness, of God (2 Cor. 4:4). He is "the visible expression of the invisible God" (Col. 1:15, Phillips), or the "exact likeness of the unseen God" (Williams). God, the invisible or unseen,

[8] Herbert E. Ryle, *The Book of Genesis* (*Cambridge Bible for Schools and Colleges*, ed. A. F. Kirkpatrick [Cambridge: The University Press, 1914]), p. 20.

8

is seen in his Son. Again, in Hebrews (1:3) it is stated that he not only reflects the glory of God but that he is the "express image of his person" (AV), "the very stamp of his nature" (RSV), "the perfect representation of His being" (Williams), or the "flawless Expression of the nature of God" (Phillips). Just as the seal on a paper or a document for an institution or agency exactly reproduces the official seal, so Jesus is the exact reproduction of the Father. He himself said, "He that hath seen me hath seen the Father" (John 14:9, AV). He prayed in his high-priestly prayer that his followers might be one, as he and his Father were one (John 17:22). They were one in purpose, motive, and will.

This One who was the "exact likeness" of the invisible God was sent into the world by the Father "in the likeness of sinful flesh" (Rom. 8:3). He was sent to do what the law could not do—set us free from the law of sin and death. When this freedom comes through union with him, we no longer walk after the flesh but after the Spirit or, as Paul expresses it in Galatians 5:16, we walk in or under the guiding impulse of the Spirit. This freedom from the law of sin and death (negative) and the freedom we have in the Spirit (positive) mean the restoration in us of the image of God which was marred by sin.

Another way of saying the same thing is to suggest that God's purpose in the union with Christ which makes us children of God is that we might be "conformed to the image of his Son" (Rom. 8:29) or that we might "bear the family likeness of His Son" (Phillips). To be conformed to the image of his Son, who was the exact reproduction of God, means to be conformed to the original image of God in man. Christ within is the only hope for the restoration of the image, which even for the child of God is only partial or incomplete in this life but which carries the promise of completeness when we shall see him as he is and awake in his likeness.

It is interesting and may be significant that God's purpose, as stated in Romans 8:29, follows immediately the great

9

promise of God, which has been such a comfort to many of God's children in times of suffering. That promise is: "And we know that all things work together ("go on working," Williams) for good to them that love God ("keep on loving God," Williams), to them who are the called according to his purpose" (Rom. 8:28, AV). All things work together for good to those who so love God and so relate themselves to his purpose that he can use their experiences to mold them more and more into the image of his Son and their Saviour. Are we so related to him? Have we discovered that not only may we learn patience through suffering but also that the burdens, the problems, the sorrows of life, if rightly accepted and interpreted, can be used by God to shape our lives increasingly into the image of our blessed Saviour and Lord?

This remaking is definitely a process. After suggesting in his great chapter on living the resurrected life that one who has been raised with Christ should set his affections on things above and should put off, or put to death, certain things, Paul then suggests that some things should be put on. In the process of becoming a new creation, a resurrected person, one strips off the old self with its practices. He puts "on the new self which is in the process of being made new in the likeness of its Creator" (Col. 3:10, Williams). Notice that it is a process. None of us has attained fully to the likeness of our Creator. But are we moving in that direction?

It is interesting to notice what follows verse 10. Using Williams' translation again, the next verse reads as follows: "In this new relation there is no Greek and Jew, no circumcised and uncircumcised, no barbarian, Scythian, slave and freeman, but Christ is everything and in us all." We can safely imply from this statement by Paul that to the degree we have progressed in the likeness of our Creator, to that degree we shall be free from class and racial consciousness and discriminations. In this new relation we shall accept one another as members of God's family. Human distinctions will be forgotten. How much have we matured as children of God? Our

10

racial attitudes may be a real barometer of our spiritual maturity.

Let us return briefly to a consideration of the image of God in man. The point of contact within man for the experience that restores the image, as suggested previously, is the image itself, admittedly marred by sin. When a person becomes a new creation through a life-changing union with Christ, the content of the original image is restored, although the shadow of sin on the image continues. The continuous nature of the influence of sin in man is one of the reasons that the image cannot be fully restored as long as man suffers the limitations of the flesh. These limitations will continue with him until the end of his earthly journey. In spite of this fact, the fellowship with God, which fallen man retained as a potentiality, becomes a reality when he is made a new creation in Christ Jesus. The image for the child of God not only represents a hunger for communion with God but in its restored form means actual communion with God, which becomes a significant, possibly the most significant, experience in the Christian's life.

It may seem paradoxical, but the hunger continues. The difference, however, is that after union with Christ, which makes us new creatures, the hunger is not for the restoration of that which has been lost or seriously marred by sin. Rather, the hunger is for a deeper and a more constant fellowship with God, for a closer walk with him under the guiding impulse of his Spirit. If we do not have such a hunger, it may be questionable whether we are children of God. It is as natural for one who has been born from above to have a hunger for spiritual food, which comes from communion with God, as it is for the babe to desire physical food. In turn, this communion with God cannot be as real and meaningful as he would have it to be unless we honestly seek to know and to do his will in every area of life. This necessarily includes those areas where knowing and living by the will of God is difficult or unpopular.

11

Significance of the Image

The fact that man was created in the image of God and that this image is the possession of all men regardless of condition, class, or color, and the companion fact that Christ died for all men give to man his worth, value, and dignity. Let us never forget that this worth and dignity applies to man as man. It is just as true of the man on one side of the tracks as on the other, of the man living in the river bottoms as on the hill, of the man in the worst slums as in the best residential area of the city.

The one covered with filth, whose body is infected with disease and whose mind is stultified with drink or dope, was created in the image of God, and Christ died to restore that image in him. We could search the world over, but we could not find a man so low, so degraded, or so far below the social, economic, and moral norms that we have established for ourselves that he had not been created in the image of God and had not been included in the blessed "whosoevers" of the redeeming gospel of Christ. The blackest child in the deepest heart of Africa was created in the image of God just as your child or mine. Furthermore, Christ died for him just as definitely as he died for you or me. This means that in God's sight the African child is as valuable as you or I or our children.

Man, as such, is worth more than all things material. It was Jesus who asked: "What will it profit a man, if he gains the whole world and forfeits his life? Or what shall a man give in return for his life?" (Matt. 16:26). If we had some old-fashioned scales, similar to those still used in some sections to weigh cotton in the field, and if we could place the entire material world on one end of the scales and one human being on the other end, the latter would more than balance the former.

The theory or doctrine of the high value of man is of importance to democracy, as well as to the Christian movement.

It is doubtful if there is any one concept more basic for democracy and Western civilization in general. Let us repeat that the high value of man is derived from his relation to God. It does not reside in him apart from God. Divorce man from God and you separate him from his source of value, and sooner or later he will lose respect for himself and for his fellow men. The extreme inhumanity of man to man characteristic of recent years has resulted from such a divorcement.

This divorcement, so prevalent in the contemporary period, may have stemmed from several things, but certainly one factor of major proportion has been man's tendency to exalt himself to the place that belongs to God. There has been some evidence of this even in the contemporary racial controversy.

In contrast, if we retain a deep conviction that men are created in the image of God and that Christ died for all, then we shall treat all men with respect. We shall recognize them as equals. We shall consider them actual or potential children of God. To use an idea of Kant, we shall never treat a human person as a mere means or instrument but always as an end of infinite value. This will be just as true of the Chinese laundryman, the Mexican laborer, or the Negro yardman or maid as it is of one's husband or wife, one's son or daughter. One is created in the image of God just as much as the other. The soul of one is just as precious in the eyes of God as that of any other. Christ died just as definitely for one as for the other.

Incidentally, the effectiveness of our service for God and our fellow man can be measured to no small degree by whether or not we consider people of value within themselves. If we see people through the eyes of God, we shall love them and respect them simply because they are people. Our capacity to love is not only a measure of our kinship to God but also a determiner, to a considerable degree, of our ability to lift people toward God.

We cannot love any as we should, in the deepest and full-

13

est sense, unless we love all people as we should, regardless of race or class. How much are we like God, who so loved that he gave his only Son that we and others might not perish but have eternal life, not only eternal in time but also in quality? This eternal life results from our union with the eternal Person. As we let him live in us, we shall reveal in our attitudes and actions his spirit and shall demonstrate his teachings. The more fully the original image of God is restored in us, the more fully we shall recognize the image of God in all men.

While making a tour of certain Latin American mission fields, I heard many wonderful reports and stories about a particular missionary. He was loved and respected by fellow missionaries and by the people among whom he lived. He filled an important place of service. When I visited the city where he lived, I saw him at various times performing the many responsibilities of his very busy life. He was efficient, but I did not discover in his regular tasks the real source of his greatness.

That was revealed one day when he and I went with some Christian young people into one of the slum areas of his city. The young people had a meeting with the children of the slums—singing hymns, telling Bible stories, and using some visual aids. Some of the children were clean and tidy, while others were dirty and filthy. Some were white, others were colored. After the meeting the children gathered outside. I saw this missionary, a graduate of a great university and with a doctor's degree from an accredited seminary, stoop down and put his arms around two of the little boys. I am persuaded that there was the main secret of his effectiveness as God's missionary. He saw in these children individuals created in the image of God, youngsters for whom Christ had died. He loved them and had respect for them simply because they were human beings.

Let us close this chapter by repeating a question asked by David Cairns and then adapt and apply it to the present racial situation. Cairns' question is, "Will mankind, in its future development, declare itself for or against man?" [9] Communism theoretically declares itself for man, but it is not man as a creation of God. Rather, it is man as a creation of material forces. The individual is lost in the mass. He has value only as he serves the purposes of the Party. He is an instrument to be used as the Party sees fit. In contrast, the Christian movement declares itself for man, for the individual man rather than the mass man of communism. The individual person from the Christian perspective is of infinite value. Let us remember, however, that Christianity declares itself for man because it first of all declares itself for God.

To apply Cairns' question personally, are we for or against man? Can we truly declare ourselves for man and at the same time declare ourselves against any man because of his race, class, or color? Can we violate the image of God in any man without really declaring ourselves against the innate dignity and worth of man, which are derived from the fact that he was created in the image of God? When one declares himself against those created in the image of God, does he not declare himself against God?

[9] David Cairns, *The Image of God in Man* (London: SCM Press, 1953), p. 249.

II

"OF ONE"

*And he made of one every nation of men to dwell
on all the face of the earth, having determined their
appointed seasons, and the bounds of their habitation.* ACTS 17:26, ASV

This verse of Scripture is used rather generally by
both the opponents and the defenders of racial segregation.
The opponents of compulsory segregation ordinarily use the
first portion of the verse, "he made of one . . . ," while the
defenders of segregation use the latter part of the verse,
"having determined . . . the bounds of their habitation."
To interpret correctly any Scripture we must consider it in its
context and interpret it in the light of the totality of Scripture. Other Scriptures frequently throw a great deal of light
on a particular statement or verse. Any interpretation that
runs counter to the general impact of the Scriptures quite
evidently is wrong.

This verse was a portion of Paul's sermon, or of the brief of
his sermon, to the Athenians on Mars' Hill. He was speaking
to a very proud people, who made a sharp distinction between the Greeks and all other peoples, classifying the latter
as barbarians. Among other things, Paul said that the Athenians, the Jews, and all other peoples were from one common source. He suggested that there was no basis for any
one group of people to feel that they were superior to all
others. The truths that Paul preached that day are relevant
for our day and every day.

One Father

There are two major views concerning the meaning of the
words "of one" in Paul's statement. One view is that the ref-

erence is to God. This would mean that all peoples and nations are from God, that they are equally his creation. The other view, held by most New Testament scholars and to be discussed later, is that the "one" refers to one human source for all the peoples and nations of the world. Williams and' Phillips both translate the expression "from one forefather."

Regardless of which view or idea is correct, Paul's sermon stressed the oneness of God and the unity of mankind. The God who created the world and everything in it is the Lord of heaven and earth. Such a God could not be contained in a temple; neither could he be worshiped or served by the hands of men. He is the one who gives life and all that is necessary to life. It was from that kind of background that Paul said, "And he made of one . . ."

The God who is the creator of the world and of man and all things that live in the world also is revealed in the Bible as Father. The idea of the fatherhood of God is much more prevalent in the New Testament than in the Old Testament, although the concept is not entirely lacking in the latter. For example, in a rather lengthy poem or song, attributed to Moses, we find the following questions:

> Do you thus requite the Lord,
>   you foolish and senseless people?
> Is not he your father, who created you,
>   who made you and established you? (Deut. 32:6).

Here Moses refers to God as Father in the sense that he was creator.

Isaiah reveals a somewhat deeper insight into the fatherhood of God as related to his people. He says:

> For thou art our Father,
>   though Abraham does not know us
>   and Israel does not acknowledge us;
> thou, O Lord, art our Father,
>   our Redeemer from of old is thy name (63:16).

17

Again Isaiah says:

> Yet, O Lord, thou art our Father;
> we are the clay, and thou art our potter;
> we are all the work of thy hand (64:8).

In a rather plaintive tone Jeremiah represents God as saying to the land of Judah:

> I thought
> how I would set you among my sons,
> and give you a pleasant land,
> a heritage most beauteous of all nations.
> And I thought you would call me, My Father,
> and would not turn from following me (3:19).

In addition to other direct references to God as Father there are many passages in the Old Testament where his fatherhood is implied. He is the Father of the fatherless (Psalm 68:5). "As a father pities his children, so the Lord pities those who fear him" (Psalm 103:13). Israel is as a son or a child of God (Hos. 11:1) and should remember that as a father disciplines his son, so God will discipline his children (Deut. 8:5).

The emphasis Jesus gave to God as Father was one of the most distinctive elements in his teachings. James S. Stewart says that Jesus made the fatherhood of God the center of everything and that he gave to the idea of father new depth and content. "He enriched it beyond recognition. And He did that not so much by anything He said, as by the way He lived." [1] Although agreeing with Stewart's statement, we would suggest, however, that Jesus did enrich the idea of God as Father a great deal by what he said as well as by the way he lived.

Jesus used "Father" in reference to God a number of times in all of the Synoptic Gospels but most frequently in Mat-

[1] James S. Stewart, *The Life and Teachings of Jesus Christ* (London: SCM Press, 1952), p. 81.

thew's record of his life and teachings. A personal check revealed forty-two references in Matthew to God as Father. A similar check revealed that Jesus in John's Gospel used "Father" to refer to God 106 times. T. W. Manson, who found 107 such references in the Fourth Gospel, says that the expression is also found sixteen times in 1 and 2 John. He concludes that "it is the Johannine writings primarily that have made 'Father' the natural name of God for Christian people." [2]

Many of the references, sixty-six in John's Gospel, are to "the Father" and frequently refer to the first member of the Triune God in contrast to the Son and to the Holy Spirit. In some of these references the general idea of God as the father of all mankind is implied.

Jesus in referring to God also used the expression "my Father." He maintained a unique son-father relation to God. He was, and is, the Son of God in a way drastically different from anyone else. In more than one sense he can correctly be spoken of as "the only Son." You and I, however, legitimately can refer to God as "my Father." If we are children of his, we can maintain a child-father relation to him. However, God should never be considered "my Father" in a selfish, childish way. We do not have any exclusive right to God. He is no more "my Father" than he is "your Father," if you have come into his family through faith in Christ. Really, my relation to him as "my Father" will not be most meaningful unless I equally recognize him as "your Father." If he is "my Father" and "your Father," then he becomes "our Father."

There is, however, genuine consolation in times of suffering and sorrow if our relations to our Heavenly Father are on a very personal basis. The deepest suffering is always personal. The last few steps into the garden of sorrow, from the human viewpoint, must be taken alone. What a source of

[2] T. W. Manson, *The Teaching of Jesus* (Cambridge: The University Press, 1948), p. 99.

strength and comfort in such times to be able to look up into the face of God and say "my Father." We can feel underneath the everlasting arms (Deut. 33:27). We can hear the familiar words: "The Lord is my shepherd" (Psalm 23:1); "My grace is sufficient for you" (2 Cor. 12:9); "Come to me, all who labor and are heavyladen, and I will give you rest" (Matt. 11:28). An examination of the life of Jesus will reveal that the expression "my Father" was frequently on his lips in his times of deepest need, such as the Gethsemane experience (Matt. 26:36–56) and in the intimate, personal discussions he had with his disciples in the hours immediately preceding his arrest, trial, and crucifixion.[3]

Jesus not only spoke of God as "the Father" and "my Father" but also as "your Father." There are nineteen references to "your Father" in Matthew's Gospel, fifteen of these in the Sermon on the Mount, with all but four of them in chapter 6. The expression "your Father" is found in only one verse in John's Gospel, but that one time is quite important. It was in the conversation Jesus had with Mary Magdalene after his resurrection. He told her to go to his brethren and to say to them, "I am ascending to my Father and your Father, to my God and your God" (John 20:17). The God and Father of the resurrected Christ was also their God and Father.

It was in the model prayer, or the so-called Lord's Prayer, that Jesus used the all-inclusive "our Father." Luke's record of the background for the prayer reveals that as Jesus prayed, one of his disciples asked him, "Lord, teach us to pray" (Luke 11:1). We wonder if such a request was not a natural result of hearing Jesus pray. Even the most spiritually mature among us do not know how to pray as we should.

We need to learn from Jesus how to pray. We need to comprehend the all-inclusiveness of genuine prayer. There is nothing narrow and selfish about prayer when it is under the

---

[3] See particularly John 14 and 15. "The Father" or "my Father" is found twenty times in John 14 alone, more than in any other chapter in the New Testament.

guidance of the Holy Spirit. One of the chief lessons to learn is to understand the depth and breadth of the expression "our Father." The "our" of the original prayer included Jesus and the disciples. Today it would include all who know Christ as Saviour and Lord, and hence all who know God as Father.

Have we let the Spirit of Christ so live in us and so deepen and expand our love for men that we can pray understandingly "our Father"? Can we pray "our Father" with a Methodist, a Presbyterian, a Pentecostal? Do we remember when we pray "our Father" that there are people living in the shacks "down by the tracks" and in the mansions on the hill who likewise pray "our Father"? Do we include them in our Christian family circle? Are we big enough and Christian enough to pray "our Father" with the Japanese, the Mexican, the Negro? If I cannot pray "our Father" with these, then I have not fully comprehended him as "my Father."

There is a sense in which God is the father of all men, at least in the sense that he is the creator of all and all are accountable to him; nevertheless, he is distinctly and peculiarly the Father of those who have come into his spiritual family through faith in Christ. He is the Father of *all* who believe, regardless of class or color. They can *all* pray "our Father." They are *all* in the family of God.

And although there is a sense in which God is the Father only of those who are Christians, yet he has the fatherly attitude toward all men. He wants to be their spiritual Father. It is not his will that any should perish. Furthermore, he makes his sun to rise "on the evil and on the good, and sends rain on the just and on the unjust" (Matt. 5:45). His goodness to those who are evil "is the chief element in his perfect character, the one that should be imitated by men if they would be true sons of the Father." [4] Jesus implied that his disciples will prove their kinship to their Father by loving their ene-

[4] Walter T. Conner, *Christian Doctrine* (Nashville: Broadman Press, 1937), p. 30.

mies and praying for those who persecute them. If our Heavenly Father would have us love our enemies, what would he have us do about those of other classes and races who are not our enemies but our brothers in Christ?

It is possible that we have argued too much about, and have been too afraid of, the doctrine of the universal fatherhood of God and brotherhood of man. Whatever may be the correct interpretation of the fatherhood-brotherhood concept, it would not justify us in being less than Christian in our relations to our Christian brothers of other races. Also, every human person should be treated by a child of God as an actual or a potential brother in Christ. Just as God reveals the fatherly attitude toward all, even those outside his spiritual family, so we his children should show the brotherly attitude toward all, even those who may not be our spiritual brothers.

Georgia Harkness suggests that it is time we quit talking so much about God as Father and began to act like he is. She further says that if we could see every person as God's child and our brother, and if this concept or attitude could become second nature to us, it "would be about the most revolutionary thing that could happen to our society." [5] We might want to insert the word "potential" before "child" and "brother" in the preceding, but to do so would not change the validity of Miss Harkness' conclusion. The effect would still be revolutionary and nowhere more so than in the area of race relations.

The latter part of Acts 17:26 is cited frequently by the defenders of present racial patterns. This portion of the verse says that God has determined the "allotted periods" ("the appointed times," Williams) of the nations of men and has set "the boundaries of their habitation" ("the limits of their lands," Williams). What does this mean? Consideration of the major emphasis of the entire sermon might help to decide

[5] Georgia Harkness, *The Modern Rival of the Christian Faith: An Analysis of Secularism* (New York: Abingdon-Cokesbury Press, 1952), p. 192.

what Paul meant by this portion of it. The most evident emphasis in the sermon was to stress or exalt the sovereignty of God. The latter portion of verse 26 underscores this emphasis. There Paul suggests that God has fixed both the seasons or time of the prosperity of the nations "and the limits of their territory." [6] He is the one who determines the destiny of each nation, Greek or barbarian, "according both to its duration in *time* and to its extension in *space*." [7]

The purpose of all of this is seen in verse 27—"that they should seek God, in the hope that they might feel after him and find him." "Feel after him" seems to describe the "motions of a blind man who gropes along after an object in the dark." [8] The purpose God had in mind in the blessings that he gave to the different peoples and nations was that they might "contemplate his wisdom in his works, and thus come to a knowledge of his existence and character." [9] In other words, his purpose, even in the exercise of his sovereign control of the nations, was and is redemptive.

Meyer suggests that the "great thought of the passage is simply: God the *Author,* the *Governor,* and the *End* of the world's history: *from* God, *through* God, *to* God." [10]

Just as God was the creator of all, so he was and is the controller of all. Neither Athenians nor any other group should get an exalted idea of the place they fill in the world and in the purposes of God. There are few things more dangerous to a nation, a racial group, or a religious denomination than for it to develop a Messiah complex. There is a fine line of distinction, but a valid one, between a deep, healthy

[6] Horatio B. Hackett, *A Commentary on the Acts of the Apostles* (*An American Commentary on the New Testament,* ed. Alvah Hovey [Philadelphia: American Baptist Publication Society, 1882]), p. 207.

[7] H. A. W. Meyer, *The Acts of the Apostles,* trans. Paton J. Gloag (New York: Funk & Wagnalls Co., 1883), p. 335.

[8] Hackett, *op. cit.,* p. 207.

[9] Albert Barnes, *Acts of the Apostles* (*Notes on the New Testament,* ed. Robert Frew [Grand Rapids: Baker Book House, 1950]), III, 263.

[10] Meyer, *op. cit.,* p. 335.

sense of divine mission and a Messiah complex or a feeling that one is the elect of the Lord, destined by him to fight his battles and to save his cause. No nation, race, or people has a corner on God. He is not a racial, national, or denominational deity. He is the God of all peoples and races. His word is the final one in every phase and realm of life. He determines when and how long a nation or a people will flourish. This is as true of those who seem to be favored as it is of the less favored.

One Family

Let us again consider, from a slightly different perspective, the expression "of one" in Paul's sermon at Mars' Hill. As suggested previously, most New Testament scholars agree that the "of one" refers to one family stock or source. W. O. Carver says, "He made of (out of) one common stock every nation (racial section) of men." [11] Lenski similarly states, "The entire human race in all its different nations sprang from one man." [12]

Barnes suggests that "this passage affirms that all the human family are descended from the same ancestor," and from this fact he concludes that "the whole human family, however they may differ in complexion, customs, and laws, are to be regarded and treated as brethren." He further says, "It follows, also, that no one part of the race has a right to enslave or oppress any other part, on account of difference of complexion." [13]

Whatever may be the correct translation or interpretation of the expression "of one," the statement by Paul clearly emphasizes the unity of the human race. There is a sense in which we are one family. We are all descendants of Adam

[11] William Owen Carver, *The Acts of the Apostles* (Nashville: Broadman Press, 1916), p. 179.
[12] R. C. H. Lenski, *The Interpretation of the Acts of the Apostles* (Columbus: Wartburg Press, 1944), p. 728.
[13] Barnes, *op. cit.*, p. 262.

and Eve; or if we want to begin with the Flood, we are all of the family of Noah. There is one common source for the human family, with all its races and nations. Modern science supports this biblical concept. For example, Ruth Benedict and Gene Weltfish say, "The Bible story of Adam and Eve, father and mother of the whole human race, told centuries ago the same truth that science has shown today: that all the peoples of the earth are a single family and have a common origin." [14]

Just as God is, in a special sense, the Father of those who are in his spiritual family, so there is a unique sense in which those of us who know him spiritually as our Father are in one family. This is the highest type of family unity. It is inner and spiritual. In this spiritual family, however, God is no respecter of persons. He is the Father of all who believe, of all who have accepted the universal invitation to come unto Christ. From his viewpoint there is no racial discrimination in his family. There should not be any by his children. These ideas, known by all Christians, have tremendous implications for human relations in general and for race relations in particular.

Those of us who have come into the family of God through a vital life-changing union with the living Christ are brothers in Christ. We are sons of the same Father. "He destined us in love to be his sons through Jesus Christ" (Eph. 1:5). This sonship comes through faith (Gal. 3:26). And because we are sons, "God has sent the Spirit of his Son into our hearts, crying, 'Abba! Father!' " Paul then adds, "So through God you are no longer a slave but a son, and if a son then an heir" (Gal. 4:6–7; cf. Rom. 8:15–16). We, along with all others who believe, are sons of the King! Our kinship with one another is basically spiritual. It was Jesus who said, "Whoever does the will of God is my brother, and sister, and mother" (Mark 3:35).

[14] *The Races of Mankind,* Public Affairs Pamphlet No. 85 (New York: Public Affairs Committee, 1951), p. 3.

There is no real solution for the race problem or any other basic human problem apart from the family spirit, which stems from the unity of God, who is our Father and who is redemptive in his purposes. The closing clause of Galatians 3:28 is as follows: "For you are all one in Christ Jesus." The "you" is emphatic in the original, and the oneness in Christ includes Jew and Greek, slave and free, male and female. These were the three great lines of cleavage in the New Testament days: race (Jew and Gentile), social status (bond and free), and sex (male and female). "One in Christ" is our hope for unity. We "are one body in Christ" (Rom. 12:5); it is Christ who "has broken down the dividing wall of hostility" between Jew and Gentile, "that he might create in himself one new man in place of the two, so making peace," that he might reconcile "both to God in one body through the cross, thereby bringing the hostility to an end" (Eph. 2:14–16). We have been "baptized into one body—Jews or Greeks, slaves or free—and all were made to drink of one Spirit" (1 Cor. 12:13). Here is our hope for breaking down the hostility between races.

The only fear is that those who have come into God's spiritual family and have drunk of the one Spirit will not let that Spirit have his way in their lives. They may let human divisions take the place of oneness in the Spirit. Possibly we should add that there is no sound hope for the solution of the major problems of mankind outside of the Christian spirit. Communism claims to have the solution, but it does not. It is a false hope. Human problems cannot be solved without the spirit of love and brotherhood. On the other hand, there is no real basis for love and brotherhood apart from a faith in, and a vital relation to, the living God, and communism has no place for God in its scheme of things.

Brothers should love one another. This should be true regardless of who those brothers are, where they live, what they have, or the race to which they belong. What a difference it would make if all of us as Christians—white, Negro,

Mexican, Japanese, and others—would apply the teachings of the Bible in our relations with one another! Paul admonished the Christians at Rome to "let love be genuine" ("let us have no imitation Christian love," Phillips). Is any of our love pretended, insincere, an imitation of the real thing? Paul adds, "Love one another with brotherly affection; outdo one another in showing honor" ("let the other man have the credit," Phillips) (Rom. 12:9–10). A little further on there is an admonition that is good for all of us: "Do not be haughty, but associate with the lowly; never be conceited" (Rom. 12:16). Phillips translates this statement as follows: "Don't become snobbish but take a real interest in ordinary people." The words that follow might also apply to some of us: "Don't become set in your own opinions. Don't pay back a bad turn by a bad turn, to *anyone*."

As those who are free in Christ, we should "honor all men" (1 Peter 2:17), or "have respect for everyone," and "love the brotherhood." Brotherly affection should supplement or be added to faith, virtue, knowledge, self-control, steadfastness, and godliness. It stands next to love in the great ladder of Christian virtues (2 Peter 1:5–7). The writer to the Hebrews admonished those to whom he wrote, "Let brotherly love continue" (Heb. 13:1). Does our "brotherly love" stand the racial test?

It might be wise for all of us to remind ourselves that Jesus plainly taught that no man can be right with God and wrong with his fellow man. We see this in the two great commandments: love God supremely and love thy neighbor as thyself. These two belong together. They stand or fall together. We see the same general emphasis in the prayer Jesus taught his disciples to pray, and particularly in the comment that was made concerning one petition in the prayer. That petition was, "And forgive us our debts, as we also have forgiven our debtors" (Matt. 6:12). This is the only petition commented on, and the statement concerning it is as follows: "For if you forgive men their trespasses, your heavenly Father also will forgive you; but if you do not forgive men their trespasses, neither will your Father forgive your trespasses" (Matt. 6:14–15).

When comparing his principles with the Old Testament Law and the Jewish interpretation of the Law, Jesus said: "You have heard that it was said to the men of old, 'You shall not kill; . . .' But I say to you that every one who is angry with his brother shall be liable to judgment; whoever insults his brother shall be liable to the council, and whoever says, 'You fool!' shall be liable to the hell of fire" (Matt. 5:21–22). Even if "brother" is restricted to our spiritual brother, he does not have to be of our national or racial group. We should be careful about our attitude toward him and what we call him.

Jesus further adds a searching statement: "If you are offering your gift at the altar, and there remember that your brother has something against you, leave your gift there before the altar and go; first be reconciled to your brother, and then come and offer your gift" (Matt. 5:23–24). The strong implication is that the worshiper's gift was not acceptable to God until he had made things right with his fellow man. What if next Sunday morning everyone in our church worship service followed literally this admonition? Would the preacher have a congregation left in the pews? And we might add, "Would there be a preacher in the pulpit?"

It should give us some concern that to the sheep and the goats the word was, "Truly, I say to you, as you did it [or "did it not"] to one of the least of these my brethren, you did it [or "did it not"] to me" (Matt. 25:40, 45). Surely we do not need to remind ourselves again that the "brethren" are all who have come into the family of God. What is our attitude toward, and our relation to, some of the least of the brethren? To be unbrotherly, particularly in relation to our spiritual brothers, may be "to discriminate more against our brother's Creator than against our brother." Is God pleased if we reject those he has accepted as his children?

One Question

This emphasis on one "Father" and one "family" creates some very real problems or questions for some people. In this chapter we shall consider only two closely related questions, which are: "How is all this related to intermarriage?" with the companion question, "What about intermarriage—is it wise or unwise?" Many who are asking these questions are good Christian people.

Let us consider briefly the second of these questions. "Is it wise for Negroes and whites to marry?" The vast majority of both Negroes and white people would answer no. It is not good common sense to cross over the color line, or many other lines, to marry.

It is also true that marriage, particularly for a child of God, is not exclusively a personal affair. Society and the institutions of society have a stake in his marriage. He should consider the effects of his marriage on his family, his community, his church, and the cause of Christ in general. If by entering into a particular marriage one would lose his opportunity to witness or to minister for Christ, or if his marriage would handicap and hurt the work of Christ, then the marriage would be not only unwise but positively wrong.

Although we do not believe it is wise for Negroes and whites to marry, our objection to such intermarriage should not be because we consider the Negro innately inferior. Many other mixed marriages—racial and religious—generally are considered unwise. For the most part, in these cases the opposition to them is not based on any idea of superiority or inferiority but on the welfare of the ones involved in the marriage, on the difficulty of attaining a satisfactory marriage relationship, on the effects on the lives of any children born in the home, and to a degree on the possible adverse effects of the marriage on society.

Negroes, with rare exceptions, are not interested in crossing the racial line to secure a life's companion. Many of them, however, do object to the laws forbidding the marriage of whites and Negroes. They contend that those laws originally were passed and are maintained primarily because the white people consider Negroes innately inferior. What if white people were in the Negro's place—would they resent the laws?

Although the marriage of Negroes and whites is not wise, the Bible has been misinterpreted and wrongly applied by some people during the present controversy. Considerable emphasis has been given by some to the laws and regulations against intermarriage in the Old Testament.

It is true that the general emphasis of the Jews was against intermarriage. In the Pentateuch are listed seven nations (Ex. 34:12–16; Deut. 7:1–8), all in the territory given to Israel by the Lord, with whom God's people were not to enter into covenant and to whom they were not to give their sons and daughters in marriage. This opposition to intermarriage, which became unusually strong in times of national crisis, reached its zenith in the days of Ezra, Nehemiah, and the prophet Malachi. Ezra extended the prohibition provided in the Pentateuch to other nations (Ezra 9:1).

There are two or three things that should be said concerning these and other Old Testament regulations regarding intermarriage. The restrictions were primarily national or tribal and not racial. With one or two possible exceptions, differences in color were not involved. Furthermore, the main motive for the restrictions was religious, although there was an element of the national or political at times. Notice the following from Deuteronomy: "You shall not make marriages with them, giving your daughters to their sons or taking their daughters for your sons. For they would turn away your sons from following me, to serve other gods" (7:3–4). The charge in Ezra was that the people, along with their religious leaders—the priests and the Levites—had not separated themselves "from the peoples of the lands with their abominations" (9:1). One commentator says concerning this statement, "The 'abominations,' which primarily referred to

30

the immoralities of their nature worship, are here associated with the mixed marriages, since the foreign wives introduced impure forms of worship among the Israelites." [15]

Epstein says that the prohibition against intermarriage with the seven nations listed in Deuteronomy "was partly political but mainly religious," [16] without any suggestion of racial purity as a motive.[17] Neufeld, even in a more positive way, says that the prohibition of marriage with strangers in the passage in Deuteronomy was not because of an "aversion to foreigners as such," but rather that it was "a device to maintain religious exclusiveness." He concludes as follows: "The real and only purpose of this bar to marriage was to protect Israel from paganism." [18] Again he says, "The generally accepted objection to intermarriage was . . . based purely upon religious grounds." [19]

David Mace suggests that the motive behind the campaign of Ezra and Nehemiah "to establish racial endogamy is quite clear. It is the fear of idolatry creeping into the national life." [20]

Conclusion

The question of social equality and intermarriage disturbs many people, but there is a prior and a more important question for Christians, which is the most disturbing of all. That question is: What is the Christian thing to do about the whole racial situation, or what would our Heavenly Father have us to do?

[15] Herbert E. Ryle, *Ezra and Nehemiah* (*Cambridge Bible for Schools and Colleges,* ed. J. J. S. Perowne [Cambridge: The University Press, 1901]), p. 114.

[16] L. M. Epstein, *Marriage Laws in the Bible and the Talmud* (Cambridge: Harvard University Press, 1942), p. 158.

[17] *Ibid.,* p. 153.

[18] E. Neufeld, *Ancient Hebrew Marriage Laws* (New York: Longmans, Green and Co., 1944), p. 217.

[19] *Ibid.,* p. 216.

[20] David R. Mace, *Hebrew Marriage: A Sociological Study* (London: Epworth Press, 1953), p. 149.

Other questions for Christians, as they face the contemporary racial situation, are: How can we apply the spirit and the teachings of Christ to our relations with those of our own and other races? Are we going to do our best to be real Christians in our relations to all men—white and all other races? Are we going to let the resurrected Christ live more fully in us and express himself more completely through us, or are we going to be controlled in thought and action by the pressures of the areas where we live? Are we going to be prophets of God with a message from the Lord, seeking as best we can to apply his spirit and to do his will in every area of life? Let us hope and pray that at least we shall never defend in the name of the Lord conditions and practices that are evidently contrary to his will.

III

"NO RESPECTER OF PERSONS"

And Peter opened his mouth, and said, Of a truth I perceive that God is no respecter of persons: but in every nation he that feareth him, and worketh righteousness, is acceptable to him.

ACTS 10:34, ASV

In these words, the opening ones of Peter's sermon in the house of Cornelius, the apostle says, "Of a truth I perceive" ("Now I really understand," Goodspeed; "I see quite plainly," Moffatt; "I am catching on" [1]) that God "shows no partiality" ("has no favourites," Moffatt, or more literally, "is no face lifter" [2]).

This statement that God is no respecter of persons, or is impartial, is one of the most significant revelations in the Bible concerning God's attitude toward, and his relation to, men. He does not look on or judge men by the color of their skin or by their general external conditions; he looks on the heart. His relations to men are absolutely fair and unprejudiced. Since God expects his children to be like him, we should not be respecters of persons. We should be impartial; we should not play favorites.

Background for the Statement

The fact that Peter said, "Now I really understand" or "I am catching on" implies his progressive enlightenment. What

[1] Frank Stagg, *The Book of Acts* (Nashville: Broadman Press, 1955), p. 120.

[2] I am indebted to one of my teacher colleagues for the following: "The thought goes back to the ancient Near East. When a subject came to a king with a petition the king would lift his face if he granted the request. Otherwise he would keep his head lowered. With God there is only one look— the look of love toward *all men*."

led Peter to make this revolutionary statement? Certainly his vision on the housetop, which will be considered later, was an important contributor. We must go back of this experience, however, for a full background for the "no-respecter-of-persons" enunciation. It is even possible that the Old Testament provided some of that background. Peter doubtless knew well the Hebrew Scriptures.

He knew, at least theoretically, that God was revealed there as one who was impartial, who showed no respect of persons. However, the incidents immediately preceding his visit to Cornelius and now his entrance into the home of the Gentile had enabled him to understand in a real or practical way that God did not show respect of persons. No longer was the no partiality doctrine merely theoretical, although Peter did not even then fully comprehend its depth and breadth. He could only go so far as to say, "Now, I am catching on to what it really means."

What was the Old Testament background that gives some basis for an understanding of what Peter meant? The Old Testament reveals that God executes judgment or justice for the fatherless and widows and loves the stranger or sojourner, "giving him food and clothing" (Deut. 10:18). It also reveals that he "shows no partiality to princes, nor regards the rich more than the poor, for they are all the work of his hands" (Job 34:19). In warning the judges to take heed or to consider what they did, Jehoshaphat reminded them that there was no iniquity (or "perversion of justice") with the Lord, "nor respect of persons, nor taking of gifts" ("bribes," ASV) (2 Chron. 19:7, AV).

In the Hebrew Scriptures God is also portrayed as impartial in his dealings with nations. He may bless nations and groups of people to an unusual degree, but when he does, he is doing it for the good of mankind in general. He blesses them that they may be a blessing. This was true of Israel as it has been of other nations and peoples. If they fail to fulfil God's purposes for them, his judgment will come upon them. This is a great truth that nations, denominations, and even races should never forget.

Peter had had ample opportunity to learn that God was no respecter of persons, not only from the Old Testament but also from the life and teachings of Jesus. He had seen this great characteristic of God demonstrated over and over again by Jesus in his dealings with men, women, and children. "In regard to all distinctions of social rank, or wealth, or knowledge, Peter had seen in his Master that absence of 'respect for persons' which even His enemies acknowledged (Matt. xxii. 16; Luke xx. 21)." [3]

The impartiality of Jesus was manifested, at least to some degree, in the selection of the twelve, who were to form the inner circle of his disciples. Evidently Jesus did not look on the outer circumstances of these men, or he would not have selected Simon Peter. There was not much in Simon, at least on the surface, to recommend him as a trusted disciple of Jesus of Nazareth.

There were one or two incidents in Peter's relation to Jesus that may have created some problems for him as he faced the challenge to go to Cornelius, who was a Gentile. When he and the other disciples were sent out on the first preaching mission, Jesus instructed them to restrict their ministry "to the lost sheep of the house of Israel" (Matt. 10:6). (This restriction on their ministry will be discussed, in a limited way, in the next chapter.) Peter, with the other disciples, also heard Jesus rebuke the Syrophenician woman and say to her, "I was sent only to the lost sheep of the house of Israel" (Matt. 15:24). Did Jesus mean to restrict his ministry and that of his disciples, temporarily or permanently, to the Jewish people?

These incidents or statements must be interpreted in the light of the totality of the Scriptures. The restrictions Jesus

[3] E. H. Plumptre, *The Acts of the Apostles* (*A Bible Commentary for Bible Students,* ed. C. J. Ellicott [London: Marshall Brothers, Ltd.]), VII, 69.

placed on his disciples when he first sent them out, along with whatever reasons he may have had for those restrictions, should be considered in the light of the blessed "whosoevers" of the gospel.

The ultimate result of the plea of the Syrophenician woman indicates the direction in which we will find a correct interpretation of the statement by Jesus to her. Although he further said that it was not meet, or fair, to take the children's bread and throw it to the dogs, yet he commended her great faith and granted her request. That which on the surface might appear to be cruel turned out to be a test of faith.

It may be that Peter, as he stood in the house of Cornelius, saw more clearly than formerly that Jesus, who came to reveal the Father, was no respecter of persons. He was a friend of the hated publicans and sinners (Matt. 11:19), ate with them (Luke 5:29–30), and chose one of them (Levi, or Matthew) to share with him in the inner circle of his disciples. No wonder these same publicans and sinners "drew near to hear him" (Luke 15:1, AV). He even had kind words for the harlots (Luke 7:36–50), some of whom believed in and followed him.

Furthermore, Peter was acquainted with the attitude of Jesus toward, and his relations to, the Samaritans, with whom the Jews had no dealings. He was along when Jesus "had to pass through Samaria" (John 4:4), although many of the Jews, going from Galilee to Jerusalem and returning, crossed over the Jordan to avoid Samaria. Peter knew of the conversation of Jesus with the woman at the well and was present when "and Samaria" was included in the commission to the followers of Christ. But even if the "and Samaria" had not been included, he knew that the marching orders of the resurrected Christ were, "Go therefore and make disciples of all nations" (Matt. 28:19). He also knew that he and the other disciples were to be witnesses not only in Jerusalem, Judea, and Samaria but "to the end of the earth" (Acts 1:8).

Peter was acquainted with the work of Philip in Samaria. He and John were sent by the other apostles evidently to investigate the revival under Philip, who was one of the seven. Doubtless, Peter had heard about Philip's experience with the Ethiopian eunuch, who was possibly a Negro.

When we think of all this background with which Peter was acquainted, it seems that he was rather hard to convince that God was no respecter of persons. It took a special vision from God even to begin to open his mind. His mind did not fully grasp, or at least completely admit, the validity of this great truth until he stood in the presence of Cornelius and was persuaded that God was in the entire experience. Stagg suggests that Peter "yielded to the light only after the greatest pressure was brought to bear upon him. His progress was painfully slow." [4] Even then he failed on one occasion when he was under pressure to stand by the conviction he had expressed in the house of Cornelius (Gal. 2:11 ff.). Let us not be too hard on Peter, however, until we ourselves have grasped more fully and applied more consistently in our lives and in our relationships with those of other races the great truth that God is no respecter of persons.

Peter's Vision

A more immediate phase of the background for Peter's opening statement that he was beginning to understand that God did not respect persons was his vision on the housetop and, to a lesser degree, his knowledge of the revelation of God to Cornelius.

Cornelius, who was a centurion, gave alms liberally to the people and was a devout man who prayed "constantly" or with reference to everything. The Lord instructed him to send for Peter at Joppa, promising that Peter would be used of the Lord to give to Cornelius the additional light he evidently was seeking.

God, as always, was working at both ends of the line.

[4] Stagg, *op. cit.*, p. 117.

While revealing himself to Cornelius, he also was preparing Peter. The next day, as the messengers of Cornelius were on their way to Joppa, which was about thirty miles from Caesarea, Peter went up on the housetop around noon to pray. This was a regular time of prayer for the Jews, and the housetops, which were flat or slightly inclined, frequently were used for such religious purposes. Incidentally, it was on a ship from Joppa, the place where Peter was, that Jonah fled, as he thought, "from the presence of the Lord" (Jonah 1:3). In Peter God had another servant or prophet who was slow to understand that God has no racial or national prejudice.

While Peter was on the housetop, he became hungry. As he waited for dinner, "he fell into a trance," possibly an ecstatic experience similar to Paul's when he was "caught up to the third heaven" (2 Cor. 12:2). In this trance Peter saw "all manner of fourfooted beasts of the earth, and wild beasts, and creeping things, and fowls of the air" (Acts 10:12, AV) let down from heaven in a great sheet.

He heard a voice saying, "Rise, Peter; kill and eat." This was too much for Peter, the Jew, with his preconceived ideas of what was clean and unclean. He "was not hungry enough even in a trance to forget his Jewish regulations and scruples." [5]

The voice was heard again as it stated a basic principle which Peter progressively was led to see had wide implications. The statement was: "What God has cleansed, you must not call common" (or "you must stop calling common"). This was a statement that inaugurated "the grand spirit . . . of human equality." [6] The same God who had spoken to Cornelius as he prayed now spoke to the apostle in a trance.

The vision was repeated three times, possibly to make it more convincing to Peter. Although he was slow to com-

---

[5] Carver, *op. cit.*, p. 108.

[6] G. T. Stokes, *The Acts of the Apostles* (*The Expositor's Bible*, ed. W. Robertson Nicoll [Grand Rapids: Wm. B. Eerdmans Publishing Co., 1940], V, 434.

prehend its deeper truths, it made a lasting impression on him. He recited the experience on at least two occasions: in the house of Cornelius and in his defense before the church at Jerusalem (Acts 11:5 ff.). In this vision and its interpretation "the Divine resistance to natural and acquired prejudice reaches its height." [7]

As Calvin expresses it, God revealed to Peter "as in a picture, that the legal difference between the clean and unclean is abolished; whence he may gather that the wall which was heretofore between the Jews and the Gentiles is now pulled down." Calvin furthermore says that "Peter durst never have opened the gate of heaven unto the Gentiles unless God himself had made a plain way and entrance for all men, by taking away the wall of separation." [8]

It was more or less natural that Peter should be perplexed and somewhat uncertain concerning the full meaning of the vision. Did it merely apply to food or to Jewish customs in general? Was there more to it than was evident on the surface? What was God trying to tell him?

While he was wondering, he received part of the answer, which represented another step in the deepening impression that God was no respecter of persons. God revealed to Peter that he was to act upon the new insight that had come to him. The Holy Spirit revealed to him that there were three men downstairs who were seeking him. The Spirit told him: "Go down, and accompany them without hesitation; for I have sent them" (10: 20). That is the way God operates in our lives. He expects us to do something about the new truth that has come to us. God's visions include an element of command. His visions are preparatory to action. They involve a "Go ye." [9]

[7] A. C. Hervey, *The Acts of the Apostles* (*The Pulpit Commentary*, ed. Spence and Exell [New York: Funk & Wagnalls, 1892]), I, 341.

[8] John Calvin, *Commentary upon the Acts of the Apostles* (Grand Rapids: Wm. B. Eerdmans Publishing Co., 1949), I, 420.

[9] See the visions of Moses (Ex. 3:1 to 4:17); Gideon (Judg. 6:11–18); Elijah (1 Kings 19:9–18); Isaiah (Isa. 6:1–9); and Paul (Acts 9:1–9).

Peter, under the leadership of the divine Spirit, invited the messengers from Cornelius to be his guests for the night. Think of the group that stayed together that night. There were Peter, a Jew but also a disciple of Christ; the two servants of Cornelius, doubtless Gentiles; and a soldier, possibly a Roman. All of these were under the same roof in the house of Simon the tanner. Imagine what they might have talked about. Do you suppose the messengers told Peter more fully about Cornelius and the dealings of the Lord with him? Also, do you suppose Peter told them about his vision and about the power of the gospel to save? "The unifying Spirit, breaking down barriers, sweeping out prejudices, was at work more powerfully than those men knew." [10]

Peter was convinced that the Lord was in the whole affair, at least enough to act. The next day he, along with "certain brethren from Joppa," went with the messengers sent by Cornelius. The brethren from Joppa may have been taken along by Peter as defense witnesses. At least, they served that purpose later at Jerusalem.

That which Peter had heard from the messengers, along with his reception in the house of Cornelius and the latter's recital of the experiences he had had with the Lord that had led him to send for Peter, helped the apostle to understand more clearly and fully that God was no respecter of persons. This was true, although Peter did remind Cornelius and those gathered in the centurion's house that by coming into the house of a Gentile he was doing something that was unlawful for a Jew. On the other hand, he now had enough insight into the meaning of his vision on the housetop that he could say that God had taught him "not to call any man vulgar or ceremonially unclean" (Williams).

In the light of the continually fuller revelation to Peter, it was more or less natural that the first words of his sermon should be, "Now I really understand" (or "I am now fully

<hr/>

[10] G. Campbell Morgan, *The Acts of the Apostles* (New York: Fleming H. Revell Co., 1924), p. 272.

convinced") "that God shows no partiality." Lenski in his commentary suggests that the expression could be translated, "Of a truth I am comprehending (a simple progressive present) that God is not a respecter of persons." [11] In one sense Peter had known for a long time that God was no respecter of persons. He had known this, however, in the same way we know many things. He knew it from the purely intellectual, theoretical viewpoint. It had never been translated into practical daily experience. He believed it with the "topside of his mind" but not in the depths of his soul. It had not become a living reality to him. It is even possible that Peter, along with the other disciples, had failed to see the relevance of the all-inclusive Great Commission to the Jewish-Gentile problem of that day.

Similarly, it seems that some conscientious Christians never have realized that some of the most basic Christian principles, which they accept as theoretically valid, apply to the contemporary racial situation. There is less excuse for us in our day to fail to comprehend the full meaning of the great truth stated by Peter, along with other fundamental Christian principles. We have the record of what Jesus did and taught. We have the epistles of Paul and the general epistles. We have the advantage of the accumulated experience of the Christian centuries.

There are some Christians even today who seek to prove from the Scriptures that the Negro is destined by God to be subservient to the white man and is supposed permanently to fill a place of secondary status in society. How unfortunate for any Christian to take such a position! Stagg suggests that "it is possible that future historians may declare the irony of ironies—that in the middle of the twentieth century, fight promoters and baseball managers did more for emancipating the Negro than did the churchmen." He then adds: "To say that these have done it for money removes none of the

---

[11] Lenski, *op. cit.*, p. 418.

sting, for it is a humiliation if a pagan for money effects good which a Christian fails to effect for love." [12]

One of the main hopes for progress in our churches and in society in general is that more and more of us will be able to say with Peter, "Now I really understand that God is no respecter of persons, that he shows no partiality." He looks on the heart. He judges by the intrinsic worth of the individual, and in his eyes all are equally created in the image of God. He does not evaluate men by the class to which they belong, the work they do, what they have, or the color of their skin. He evidently does not think of them as belonging to some particular race. For him they are all members of the human race. We should look on men through the eyes of our Heavenly Father. His children should give indication of their kinship to him by showing no partiality. May the Lord help every one of us to make progress in that direction.

Significance of the Principle

As mentioned, the statement that God was no respecter of persons was the opening sentence of Peter's sermon, or of a digest or synopsis of his sermon, in the house of Cornelius. In the presence of Cornelius, with his loved ones and guests, Peter stood to proclaim the grace and goodness of God in Christ. The light of God's truth flooded his soul to a degree that he had not known before. He saw that "God does not accept a man because he is a Jew or reject him because he is a Gentile." [13] He saw that there was no class consciousness with God. Class and color lines do not belong in the realm of the Spirit.

This conviction was confirmed further before Peter completed his sermon. As he preached the good news of the gospel to them, "the Holy Spirit fell on all who heard the word"

[12] Stagg, *op. cit.*, p. 124.
[13] W. T. Conner, *The Gospel of Redemption* (Nashville: Broadman Press, 1945), p. 68.

(Acts 10:44). This was the final testimony that God was no respecter of persons. Those who had come with Peter from Joppa "were amazed." The outpouring of the Spirit was sufficient proof to them that God was impartial.

It seems that the clinching argument by Peter, when he was questioned by some of the Jerusalem brethren about going in to eat with uncircumcised men, was the fact that as he spoke the Holy Spirit fell on those present as he had upon Peter and the others "at the beginning." He then asked the searching question, "Who was I that I could withstand God?" The record says, "When they heard this they were silenced" (Acts 11:17–18).

Could it be that the movement of the masses around the world in our day is of the Lord? Is it possible that any opposition to their efforts to move upward and to improve their status is really opposition to God?

The fact that Peter was questioned by some of the brethren of the Jerusalem church would indicate that they recognized the significance of the Cornelius experience. Also, their question was one concerning Peter's violation of a social custom or taboo. The no-respecter-of-persons principle does not apply exclusively to the spiritual realm. It had tremendous social consequences in Peter's life and will have them in our lives, if it really permeates our souls.

It is quite apparent that the early followers of Christ recognized the importance of the no-respecter-of-persons principle. It is repeated specifically a number of times in the New Testament, while the general idea permeates all of the New Testament. Peter himself obviously never forgot the opening words of his sermon in the house of Cornelius. We find him saying in his first epistle: "And if you invoke as Father him who judges each one impartially ("without respect of persons," AV) according to his deeds, conduct yourselves with fear throughout the time of your exile" (1 Peter 1:17). The God we worship is Father, but his fatherhood does not exclude the idea of judgment. Lenski correctly sug-

43

gests that God is not "an indulgent grandfather who shuts an eye to the sins of his children." [14]

God's children can be assured, however, that God judges every man without partiality or favoritism. He "is not influenced in his treatment of men by a regard to rank, wealth, beauty, or any external distinction." [15] "Any external distinction" would include color. We cannot imagine God's making any difference in the treatment of his children on the basis of the pigmentation of their skin. This is unthinkable. Should it not also be unthinkable of those who claim to be his children?

This idea of the impartiality of God is quite prominent in the epistles of Paul. It might properly be considered the central theme of the first chapters of Romans. In these chapters Paul says that all men, Jews and Gentiles, are under condemnation for sin. God has provided a way of salvation, which will bring freedom from the enslavement of sin and from the condemnation of the law and will bring into the family of God those who will accept that way. This salvation, with its attendant blessings, is offered to both Jews and Gentiles. The faith that brings salvation is a great common denominator.

The no-respecter, or no-partiality, principle is stated explicitly by Paul in the second chapter of Romans. He opens the chapter with the broad statement, "Therefore you have no excuse, O man, whoever you are." Later he says, "For he [God] will render to every man according to his works" (v. 6). Then he closes the section with the great summary statement, "For God shows no partiality" ("for there is no respect of persons with God," ASV).

This statement by Paul was in rather sharp contrast to the common Jewish attitude. They fancied that they had a con-

[14] R. C. H. Lenski, *The Interpretation of the Epistles of St. Peter, St. John and St. Jude* (Columbus, Ohio: Lutheran Book Concern, 1938), p. 59.
[15] Albert Barnes, *The General Epistles of James, Peter, John, and Jude*, p. 145.

siderable monopoly on the divine favor. They were not the last, and possibly not the first, to think that they were the elect of the Lord. One of the besetting temptations of a favored people has always been the development of a Messiah complex. It is a danger to religious bodies as well as to nations and races. Everyone needs to try to see himself impartially, as God sees him.

Paul suggests that the Jew may be first in glory and honor (v. 10), but he is also first in tribulation and distress (v. 9). This merely may mean that those who have been favored have an additional responsibility. Whatever is the correct interpretation, it certainly means that God shows no partiality. There is always a redemptive purpose in any special favor or blessing he gives to an individual or group. We can be sure that he judges men "as they *ought* to be judged; according to their *character* and deserts; and not contrary to their character, or by partiality."[16] Calvin suggests that God has "no respect for those things which are wont to be highly valued by men, such as kindred, country, dignity, wealth, and similar things." He then concludes that "respect of persons is to be here taken for the distinction or the difference there is between one nation and another."[17]

It has already been implied that the impartiality of God does not limit his sovereignty. He may give to some special favors, "but he shows no capricious partiality, always, in his final judgment, holding an even balance between responsibilities and privileges."[18]

Paul applies the no-partiality doctrine in several ways and to various areas of human relations. In defending his apostleship in the Galatian letter, he mentions the approval of the pillars of the church at Jerusalem—James and Cephas and

[16] Albert Barnes, *Romans* (*Notes on the New Testament,* ed. Robert Frew [Grand Rapids: Baker Book House, 1950]), IV, 58.

[17] Calvin, *The Epistles of Paul,* p. 94.

[18] Albert N. Arnold and D. B. Ford, *Commentary on the Epistle to the Romans* (*An American Commentary on the New Testament,* ed. Alvah Hovey [Philadelphia: American Baptist Publication Society, 1889]), p. 67.

John—but inserts the following in parenthesis: "What they were makes no difference to me; God shows no partiality" (Gal. 2:6). Their reputation, in a sense, was really immaterial to Paul. God had not been partial to them. He had revealed himself to Paul as well as to them.

Paul also applies the great principle to human relations in general. The application is found in Galatians 3:28, which has been quoted previously. Williams' translation reads as follows: "There is no room for Jew or Greek, no room for slave or freeman, no room for male or female, for you are all one through union with Christ Jesus." [19]

Notice the background of Galatians 3:28. In verse 26 Paul had said, "In Christ Jesus you are all sons of God, through faith." We come into the family of God through faith. That is true of Jew and Gentile, slave and free, male and female. Such faith puts all on the same level. Following faith comes baptism (v. 27), when believers put on Christ, or clothe themselves with Christ (Williams). This is also true of all who are in Christ. It is said that on the same day that Charles Evans Hughes, who was at that time the chief justice of the Supreme Court of the United States, presented himself for membership in the Calvary Baptist Church of Washington, D. C., a Chinese laundryman came down another aisle to join the church. The pastor is reported to have said, "The ground around the cross is wondrously level." Whether or not this incident literally happened, the principle stated is true.

Do you suppose if Paul were living today that he would apply the no-partiality principle to the great divisions that tend to plague our contemporary society? We believe he would. We believe that he would say to us: "There is neither Russian nor American, there is neither male nor female, there is neither employer nor employee, there is neither white nor Negro, but you are all one in Christ Jesus."

[19] For other references with the same general emphasis in Paul's epistles see Rom. 10:12; 1 Cor. 12:13; and Col. 3:11.

Application of the Principle

Most Christians see clearly that the no-respecter-of-persons principle applies to the spiritual area. They believe that all men are without excuse, that they have had enough light from God to be responsible to him. This means that all are under condemnation for sin. It is also true that most Christians agree that God has provided one plan for the salvation of all people and that this way of salvation is equally open to all. Not only have all sinned and fallen short of the glory of God (Rom. 3:23), but it is just as true that the gospel is "the power of God for salvation to every one who has faith" (Rom. 1:16).

Every invitation to salvation in the Old and New Testaments is to all men. Isaiah, "the Prince of Old Testament Prophets," sounded the universal call:

> Ho, every one who thirsts, come to the waters;
> and he who has no money, come, buy and eat!
> Come, buy wine and milk without money and
> without price. ISAIAH 55:1

Jesus similarly said, "If any one thirst, let him come to me and drink" (John 7:37). John, in Revelation, possibly deliberately used the same symbol: "Let him who is thirsty come, let him who desires take the water of life without price" (22:17).

There are many other Scriptures which express in different ways the universal invitation—an invitation which proves without any doubt that God is no respecter of persons. It was Jesus who said, "Him who comes to me I will not cast out" (John 6:37). Peter, in his great sermon on the day of Pentecost, quoted the following from the prophet Joel: "Whoever calls on the name of the Lord shall be saved" (Acts 2:21; cf. Rom. 10:13).

Does the no-respecter-of-persons principle apply exclusively to the spiritual realm? There are many Christians who say that it does. They agree that God has only one plan of salvation and that it is open equally to all men of all classes and races. They contend, however, that the principle does not apply to the broader social relations. They say that it is not applicable in any way to contemporary class and racial problems.

But what does a study of Peter's vision, with his interpretation of it and his reaction to it, reveal? His vision plainly convinced him that he "should not call any man common ("vulgar," Williams) or unclean" (Acts 10:28).

What effect did this lesson have on Peter? It caused him, as suggested previously, to violate some of the customs, mores, and taboos of his society. He invited the men sent by Cornelius, who were doubtlessly Gentiles, "in to be his guests" (Acts 10:23). He went into the house of Cornelius, which he himself said was unlawful for a Jew to do (Acts 10:28). Some of the members of "the circumcision party" in the Jerusalem church asked him the pointed question, "Why did you go to uncircumcised men and eat with them?" (Acts 11:3). It is even possible that Peter acceded to the request of Cornelius and his friends and remained with them "for some days" (Acts 10:48).

The preceding may be disturbing to some Christians of the white race, but let all of us sincerely search for the fullest implications of the no-respecter-of-persons principle and of other great truths that are an integral part of the gospel we preach, teach, and profess to follow. If God is no respecter of persons, if he shows no partiality, our ultimate goal should be the elimination of all partiality, prejudice, and discrimination from our lives. All men should be considered as of infinite worth, created in the image of God, actual or potential children of God, and as members of the human race rather than of some division within that race. These attitudes may represent a long, long step for most of us, but is it not a direction that is plainly revealed by an examination of Peter's vision and of the results in his life of that vision?

The Christians who have achieved the most worthwhile things for God and men have been those who have had visions from God and who have had the faith and courage to strive to make those visions living realities among men. May God grant that we share something of Peter's vision, grasp its deeper meaning, and have the faith in God and the stamina of soul to be obedient to the heavenly vision!

However, many of us will have some criticism and opposition if our vision of God leads us to viewpoints and positions that are contrary to the customs and traditions of our society. Some of the harshest criticism and the most active opposition may come from within the Christian group itself. This at times may be very hard to understand and even more difficult to bear.

While we should have no particular desire to be martyrs, we should not forget that as long as our society and people in general fall below God's standards, there is something wrong if all men speak well of us. Such might be an indication that we are false teachers or prophets (Luke 6:26). We cannot do what we ought to do for the Lord and please everybody, and frequently the "everybody" includes some fellow Christians and church members. In times of criticism may the conviction that God has spoken to us be deep enough that we can say, within our own hearts whether or not we ever say it publicly, "Who was I that I could withstand God?" (Acts 11:17). Let us also be careful about our personal reaction to any criticism or opposition. May we never become embittered. May we never return evil for evil. May the Lord preserve us from a self-righteous, holier-than-thou attitude. Let us never pity ourselves or develop a martyr complex.

James in his epistle applies the no-respecter-of-persons principle to the church. Before applying it specifically, he makes a general statement of it as follows: "My brothers, stop trying to maintain your faith in our Lord Jesus Christ . . . along with acts of partiality to certain ones" (James 2:1, Williams). Mayor gives the verse the following meaning:

"Do not you, who call yourselves believers in Christ, disgrace your faith by exhibitions of partiality." [20] Notice the plural—acts or exhibitions of partiality. James condemns all partiality. Such partiality, or respect of persons, was and is inconsistent with faith in Christ, who shows no partiality.

The general principle is applied by James to one particular area—the treatment by the followers of Christ of the rich and the poor in their assemblies. James follows this application with a restatement of the general principle. He then relates the principle to love for one's neighbor. It is possible that James related the principle of no respect for persons to love of a neighbor because some of those to whom he was writing had suggested that their preferential treatment of the rich, who oppressed them (2:6), was the application of the command to love one's enemy. James says, however, that if they showed partiality in that love, they committed sin (2:8–9). He also says that they violated the law as a whole when their conduct was contrary to the "spirit of the law."

Are these words from the Epistle of James relevant to our day? Do we and our churches need to hear and to heed the words of James: "Stop trying to maintain your faith in our Lord Jesus Christ along with acts of partiality to certain ones"?

The Principle and the Idea of Inferiority

How is the no-respecter-of-persons principle related to the supposed superiority and inferiority of races? The debate regarding the superiority-inferiority doctrine has been brought into sharp focus again in recent years.

Most scientific students of human life and behavior would agree with Montagu that racism, which is the idea of the innate superiority-inferiority of certain races, is man's most dangerous myth.[21] Soper says that "there is practical una-

[20] Joseph B. Mayor, *The Epistle of St. James* (Grand Rapids: Zondervan Publishing House, 1954), p. 79.

[21] M. F. Ashley Montagu, *Man's Most Dangerous Myth* (3rd ed.; New York: Harper & Brothers, 1952).

nimity of conviction that races are not inherently superior or inferior." [22] There might be found, after considerable search, some supposed scientific evidence of the superiority-inferiority doctrine.

However, from the Christian perspective, and even from the democratic viewpoint, it makes little difference whether the idea of inherent superiority or inferiority is correct or incorrect. For example, democracies, political and spiritual, are built on the idea of innate human dignity and an essential equality of all. This does not mean necessarily that all are equal in ability; it does mean that they are equally men, are equally members of the group, and are to be treated impartially.

We are not suggesting by the preceding that the Negro is by nature inferior and the white man superior. However, even if a particular race were innately and permanently superior, what would this mean from the perspective of the Christian religion and ethic? The Christian religion says the strong should serve the weak. It is a fundamental Christian principle that privilege and power are never to be used selfishly, that they always involve responsibility. Montagu, speaking as a scientist, says:

Suppose for a moment that significant differences did exist between different peoples which rendered one, in general, superior to the other; a reasonably developed human being would hardly consider such differences sufficient reason for withholding any opportunities for social and cultural development from such groups. On the contrary, he would be the more anxious to provide them with such opportunities. Undeveloped personalities operate in the opposite manner and, creating most of the differences they condemn, proceed to intensify those differences by making it more and more difficult for the groups thus treated to avoid or overcome them.[23]

[22] Edmund D. Soper, *Racism: A World Issue* (New York: Abingdon-Cokesbury Press, 1947), p. 38.
[23] *Op. cit.,* p. 119. Used by permission.

Are we "reasonably developed" human beings, or are we "undeveloped personalities" when measured by this standard? More important, are we mature or immature Christians in our relations to those of other races?

IV

"YOU ARE A SAMARITAN"

The Jews answered him, "Are we not right in saying that you are a Samaritan and have a demon?"
JOHN 8:48

It may be interesting to notice the things that Jesus had said which so enraged the Jews that they blurted out, "You are a Samaritan and have a demon."

Some of them had believed him, or believed *on* or *in* him. Jesus sought to lead them to understand the nature and results of a true faith in him. He was not satisfied with a momentary conviction. The test was whether or not they would continue "in his word."

He attempted to lead all of those who were listening to him to a proper understanding of the spiritual nature of his work and kingdom. This seemed impossible for most of them to comprehend. He spoke to them of spiritual and moral freedom; they thought in terms of political freedom. He spoke of the spiritual Israel, of the true sons of Abraham; they were concerned only with the physical and national Israel. He patiently sought to convict them of their error; they lacked either the insight or the willingness to grasp his meaning. How tragic was their spiritual blindness!

They did the thing that many people do when they are irritated by the superior spirit of another or when they cannot answer his arguments. "In their rage and fury they can think of no meaner things to say" [1] than "you are a Samaritan." It is possible that this term of reproach was meant as a sneer at

[1] A. T. Robertson, *Word Pictures in the New Testament* (Nashville: Sunday School Board of the Southern Baptist Convention, 1932), V, 155.

his visit to Samaria and his conversation with the Samaritan woman at Jacob's well.[2]

Notice in this whole incident the contrast between Jesus and the Jews. He evidently was perfectly calm, as one usually is who has the right on his side. He did not retaliate or strike back. He did not stoop to their level and use false labels. He passed by the "you are a Samaritan" charge, although he did reply to the charge of demon possession. It is possible that Jesus did not answer the first portion of the charge because he did not agree with the current Jewish appraisal of the Samaritans. To him the label was not an insult. "For Him it contained nothing offensive, for He knew that Samaritans might equal or excel Jews (iv. 39–42; Luke x. 33, vii. 16) in faith, benevolence, and gratitude."[3] He evidently thought that the best thing to do about the charge was to ignore it. This incident might have provided part of the background for Peter's statement that "when he was reviled, he did not revile in return" (1 Peter 2:23).

The Jews and the Samaritans

In the days of the divided kingdom, the city of Samaria was the capital of the Northern Kingdom. It became synonymous with the country; hence the Northern Kingdom frequently was called Samaria. The name "Samaritans" was used, at least on one occasion, to refer to the inhabitants of the Northern Kingdom (2 Kings 17:29).

When the Northern Kingdom fell, many of the people were carried off as captives. It seems that the poorer classes, however, were left behind to till the soil and to tend the vineyards. On the other hand, as was customary in those days, the Assyrian conquerors sent colonists in from the outside.

[2] A. Plummer, *The Gospel According to Saint John* (*Cambridge Bible for Schools and Colleges,* ed. J. J. S. Perowne [Cambridge: The University Press, 1889]), p. 193.
[3] *Ibid.*

These colonists, representing various peoples and areas (2 Kings 17:24), brought with them competing customs and traditions, religious and otherwise. They intermingled and evidently intermarried considerably with the Israelites who had been left behind. They became a "heterogeneous conglomerate" who "neglected the Temple and ignored the desolation of Jerusalem" [4] after the fall of Judah. During the exile they had forgotten the covenant and disregarded the Law.

In spite of all of this the religion of the Samaritans seemingly continued to be predominantly Jewish. At least, when they asked for the privilege of sharing in the rebuilding of the Temple in the days of Zerubbabel, "they claimed, apparently with a good conscience, to serve God and to sacrifice to Him as the Jews did (Ezra 4:1 f.)." [5] Whether or not their offer to help, with their attendant confession of faith, was in good conscience, their help was declined. Their offer of friendship was turned to "deadly hostility." "The old enmity between north and south no doubt intensified the quarrel, and the antagonism of Jew and Samaritan in its bitterness was destined to pass into a proverb." [6]

When the Jews refused to accept the proffered help of the people of Samaria, the latter, under the guidance of Manasseh—a priest who had been expelled from Jerusalem by Nehemiah because of his marriage to the daughter of Sanballat the Horonite (Neh. 13:28)—obtained permission from the Persian king to erect a temple on Mount Gerizim. "The new worship thus started, placed them at once in the position of a rival and schismatical sect." [7] The rivalry and hatred became very intense. Josephus, the Jewish historian, says that some of the Samaritans profaned the Temple at Jeru-

[4] H. E. Dana, *The New Testament World* (3rd ed., Nashville: Broadman Press, 1937), p. 71.

[5] W. Ewing, "Samaritans," *The International Standard Bible Encyclopaedia*, ed. James Orr (Chicago: The Howard-Severance Co., 1915), IV, 2673.

[6] *Ibid.*

[7] *The Four Gospels*, *Ellicott's Commentary on the Whole Bible*, VI, 289.

salem by throwing dead men's bodies "in the cloisters" [8] or on the sacred pavement. The vigorous reforms under Ezra and Nehemiah seem to have widened the breach between the Jews and their neighbors, particularly between them and the Samaritans.

To the Jews "Samaritan" became a term of abuse. David Smith says, "Indeed the Jews had a worse hatred of the Samaritans than of the heathen, herein exemplifying that singular fact whereto the history of religion bears abundant and deplorable witness, that quarrels are ever bitterest where differences are least and grounds of toleration most ample." [9]

Josephus says that the Samaritans claimed that they were kinsmen of the Jews when the latter were prosperous but denied such kinship in times of adversity. For example, he says,

And when they see the Jews in prosperity, they pretend that they are changed, and allied to them, and call them kinsmen, as though they were derived from Joseph, and had by that means an original alliance with them: but when they see them falling into a low condition, they say they are no way related to them, and that the Jews have no right to expect any kindness or marks of kindred from them, but they declare that they are sojourners, that come from other countries. [10]

Whether Josephus presents an accurate picture or colors it because of his Jewish prejudice, there is no doubt about the enmity between the Jews and the Samaritans in the days of Jesus. The Jews avoided all possible contacts with the Samaritans. The strength of this aversion was brought out in bold relief at Jacob's well when Jesus asked a drink of the Samaritan woman. She asked him the searching question, "How is it that you, a Jew, ask a drink of me, a woman of

---

[8] *Antiquities of the Jews*, XVIII, 2, 2.

[9] David Smith, *The Days of His Flesh* (London: Hodder & Stoughton, n.d.), pp. 73–74.

[10] *Antiquities*, IX, 14, 3; cf. XI, 8, 6 and XII, 5, 5.

Samaria?" The following statement is then added, either by the woman or, as most commentators believe, by the writer of the Fourth Gospel, as an explanation for her question: "For Jews have no dealings with Samaritans" (John 4:9).

As is usually true, the Jewish-Samaritan prejudice was not entirely one-sided. The Samaritans were strongly prejudiced also. This doubtlessly was the reason why the people of a Samaritan village refused to receive Jesus and his disciples. Luke 9:53 says that they "would not receive him, because his face was set toward Jerusalem" ("refused to welcome him because he was obviously intending to go to Jerusalem," Phillips). Jerusalem was a rival place of worship. If the Samaritans had heard of Jesus, it might have been that they had hoped that he would decide that Mount Gerizim should be the place where men should worship Jehovah. His face, however, was set toward ("His face was going to," Williams) Jerusalem. The village refused to welcome him.

Notice the contrast in the reactions of Jesus and his disciples, at least John and James, the "sons of thunder." They asked Jesus, "Do you want us to bid fire come down from heaven and consume them?" Some of their Jewish prejudice was expressed in the question. They, along with the other disciples, "were just as ready to take offence as the Samaritan villagers were to give it. The powder of national enmity was stored up in their breasts; and a spark, one rude word or insolent gesture, was enough to cause an explosion." [11] Jesus had none of their spirit. He rebuked his disciples, and with them he "went on to another village." One of these very disciples, John, after he had caught more of the spirit of his Master, went on a mission of love to Samaria (Acts 8:14–25). How much are we gripped by the spirit of narrow nationalism and rabid racialism, and how much by the spirit of the Master? Is our spirit that of the world or is it distinctly Christian?

[11] A. B. Bruce, *The Training of the Twelve* (New York: Doubleday, Doran & Co., Inc., 1929), p. 244.

Jesus and the Samaritans

Additional consideration of Jesus' attitude toward, and relation to, the Samaritans may give us some helpful ideas concerning our relations to those of other races. The Jewish-Samaritan problem was the most acute racial, national, and religious conflict of his day. It was comparable, at least in its depth and viciousness, to the Negro-white problem of the contemporary period. It seems fair to conclude that what Jesus did about the Jewish-Samaritan problem of his day he would do about the Negro-white problem of our day.

Before turning to the more positive aspects of the relation of Jesus to the Samaritans, let us consider briefly an incident that creates problems for some people. When Jesus sent out the twelve, he specifically forbade them to go to the Gentiles in general and to the Samaritans in particular (Matt. 10:5). Why this restriction, particularly in the light of the ministry of Jesus to the Samaritans (John 4:7–42), which possibly had taken place about a year before the twelve were sent out?

There are two possible explanations. One is that the good news of the Messiah was first to be presented to the Jews. They were to have the first chance to accept him. The other explanation for the prohibition, and possibly the main or correct one, was the fact that the twelve were not adequately prepared at this time "to preach the gospel, or to do good works, either among Samaritans or Gentiles. Their hearts were too narrow, their prejudices too strong: there was too much of the Jew, too little of the Christian, in their character." [12]

This limitation of their ministry should be interpreted, as is true of every specific Scripture, in the light of the totality of the Scriptures. When this is done, we are forced to conclude that whatever limitation was meant was temporary. There are countless Scriptures that prove that Christ's compassion

[12] *Ibid.*, p. 101.

and love overleaped every boundary of national hatred and every wall erected by racial prejudice.

Let us examine somewhat more in detail the experience of Jesus with the woman at the well. The record says that when he left Judea to go to Galilee, "he had to pass through Samaria" ("he must needs go through Samaria," AV). Was this primarily a geographic convenience or an inner urge or necessity? It was the shortest route. Many Jews, however, avoided passing through Samaria. Was lack of time Jesus' reason for going through Samaria? That is doubtful, since he tarried for two days in Samaria. Could it be that his decision was based on an inner compulsion?

Regardless of the reason for going through Samaria, the results were glorious. Here at Jacob's well we see demonstrated some of the most appealing and challenging traits of Jesus. He who was a master in handling a crowd was also the world's most effective personal worker. Many of his greatest lessons, demonstrating his infinite skill as a teacher, were taught to just one person. He never lost sight of the individual in the crowd. He never placed people in certain classes or pigeonholes. Every person for him was a human being of real worth and dignity. Each was an actual or a potential child of God.

The woman at the well, for Jesus, was such a human person. She was a woman,[13] a Samaritan woman, a sinful Samaritan woman, but Jesus reached across these barriers of sex, race, and moral condition to bring a blessing to her. He never permitted any division or prejudice—class, color, or creed—to keep him from meeting the spiritual needs of men and women. He introduced the Samaritan woman to the living

[13] David Smith (*op. cit.*, pp. 76–77) suggests that it was a greater wonder to the disciples that Jesus talked with a woman than that he conversed with a Samaritan. He further says that a Jew could not greet a woman nor talk with one on the street, even if she was his wife, sister, or daughter. In the morning prayer the men praised God "who hath not made me a Gentile, a slave, a woman." It was considered impious to teach the words of the Law to a woman.

water, which permanently satisfies the thirst of the human heart and which is "a spring of water welling up to eternal life!"

He also showed her, and would reveal to us, that the claims of rival sacred places—Gerizim and Jerusalem—were swept away in the revelation that God is spirit and can be worshiped anywhere. This universalizes religion. What Christ gave to the woman he gave to the human race; what she received she received for mankind.[14]

Many of the Samaritans were responsive to the woman's report that she had met and talked with the promised Messiah. They requested Jesus to tarry with them. He remained two days, and many of them believed the message he proclaimed to them. What a short time and yet how long a time for the Son of God to tarry in one village!

Think of what would be missing from the gospel story if Jesus had not stopped that day at Jacob's well. How grateful we ought to be for his ministry among the Samaritans. No wonder that the first notable revival outside of Jerusalem was among the people of Samaria (Acts 8:4–25). They had been prepared for the gospel of Christ by his visit with a Samaritan woman at Jacob's well and by his other contacts with Samaria and the Samaritans. Many of the latter doubtlessly were acquainted with his attitude toward them and his ministry to their people.

In one of his greatest parables Jesus made a Samaritan the hero (Luke 10:25–37). Jesus never did anything by accident. He deliberately selected the Samaritan to illustrate the neighborly spirit. It should be remembered also that the story was told in response to a question by a Jewish lawyer, and it can be assumed that the victim in the story was a Jew. The existence of the feud between the Jews and the Samaritans "enormously increases the point of the parable." [15]

[14] A. Fairbairn, *Studies in the Life of Christ* (London: Hodder & Stoughton, 1881), p. 127.

[15] H. K. Luce, *Luke* (*Cambridge Bible for Schools and Colleges*), p. 116.

The priest and the Levite saw the man who had been beaten by the robbers, and they passed by on the other side. In contrast, a Samaritan as he journeyed (possibly suggesting a longer trip than from Jerusalem to Jericho) did what no Jew would have expected him to do. He proved himself "a better man than the orthodox Priest and Levite"; [16] he showed "a spontaneous and perfect pity of which neither Priest nor Levite had been remotely capable." [17] He acted that day not as a Samaritan but rather as a man, as any man should act toward a fellow human being in distress. The key to what he did was the fact that he had compassion on the one who had been stripped and robbed.

Jesus pressed home the lesson of the story by asking the lawyer, "Which of these three, do you think, proved neighbor to the man who fell among the robbers?" The lawyer evidently could not get rid of all his prejudice. He could not bring himself to reply, "The Samaritan." He said, "The one who showed mercy on him." It is possible that one purpose Jesus had in telling this beautiful parable was that the lawyer and other Jews might see the foolishness and sinfulness of their prejudice against the Samaritans.

Jesus had some other contacts with Samaritans in which they were revealed in a favorable light. One such occasion was when he was passing along between Samaria and Galilee and was met by ten lepers. He told them to go and show themselves to the priests. As they went in obedience to Jesus, they were cleansed. Only one returned, a Samaritan, and fell at the feet of Jesus, thanking him for his miraculous healing. "Then said Jesus, 'Were not ten cleansed? Where are the nine? Was no one found to return and give praise to God except this foreigner?'" (Luke 17:11–18).

Even after his resurrection Jesus showed a continuing concern for the people of Samaria. He said to his disciples, "You shall receive power when the Holy Spirit has come upon you;

[16] F. W. Farrar, *Luke* in *Cambridge Bible*, p. 205.
[17] *Ibid.*, p. 206.

61

and you shall be my witnesses in Jerusalem and in all Judea and Samaria and to the end of the earth" (Acts 1:8). Why did Jesus include "and Samaria"? Would there not have been just as much reason to include Perea or Galilee? Samaria must have been deliberately included. Possibly Jesus intended to challenge the strongest prejudice of his followers of that day. What about us—do we need the message of "and Samaria"? Do we have our Samarias, our areas of prejudice? If so, Jesus would have us cross over the border. There are no national or racial lines in his Commission.

"We Are . . . You Are"

Let us return to the incident when the Jews said to Jesus, "You are a Samaritan." They had said, "We are Abraham's children." That was like saying, "We are real Jews, you are not. You are a heretic. You belong to a mongrel race."

Many interracial problems, past and present, have their roots in the "we-you" psychology. Those of the "we" group usually belong to the majority and consider themselves superior. Those of the "you" group are excluded from many of the privileges of the "we" group. They are considered inferior. They are the Samaritans, the racial and cultural minorities.

There is always a possibility that the members of a "you" group, under the continuing pressure of a dominant "we" group, may develop a deepening racial consciousness with an intense pride in the accomplishments of their race. When that happens, they tend to become a competing "we" group. They no longer are willing to accept as permanent and inevitable a secondary status in society. They challenge the majority to treat them as equals, to accept them as full partners in the culture.

When this stage is reached in the relation of two great racial groups, adjustments must be made in the previously accepted patterns, or friction and serious trouble usually will result. There is considerable evidence that this stage has arrived in the relation of the white and Negro races in the United States, both in the North and in the South. The Negroes, in the main, are more vocal and more militant than ever before. They increasingly refuse to accept the "you" group status.

A thing that tends to make the present situation even more serious is the trend among the Negroes of the United States to effect a common cause with the colored peoples of the world. Those colored peoples, along with the common people in general, are restless. They are on the move around the world. They are asking that they be treated with dignity and respect and dealt with as equals. The movement of the masses is an integral part of the world crisis or revolution, which is shaking the very foundations of Western civilization and of world civilization in general. One cannot understand present developments regarding the Negro-white problem in the United States without seeing it in the setting of a world revolution.

Regardless of how serious the present racial situation may be or may become, and regardless of whether or not it is closely related to the contemporary world crisis, this much is certainly true: the "we-you" psychology does not belong within the Christian vocabulary. The only divisions among men in a totally Christian society would be those based upon moral conduct and spiritual condition. All men would be considered actual or potential members of the family of God. Each individual would be treated as a human being, a divine creation, and as a possible brother beloved. In such an atmosphere the "we-you," the "I-belong-you-do-not," attitude could not continue.

Probing Our Prejudices

Henry Smith Leiper has an interesting little book entitled *Blind Spots*. The title is based on the fact that the retina of each eye has a blind spot. Leiper contends that most Christians have some blind spots in regard to race relations. Cer-

63

tainly few, if any, of us would say that we are entirely free from racial prejudice. At times it crops up in the most unexpected ways and frequently at the most embarrassing moments. Most of us would address at least some individuals belonging to one or more racial groups as "you are." What are those groups for you and for me?

Racial prejudice is particularly prevalent in the contemporary period. Arnold Toynbee goes so far as to say that modern Western race feeling dates from the last quarter of the fifteenth century.[18] This may be true of modern Western race feeling, but it is not true of race feeling as such. For example, there were the Greek-barbarian and the Jew-Gentile divisions in biblical times. It is true, however, that modern race and color prejudices were greatly heightened, if not created, by the discovery of America and the establishment of trade routes to India. Also, prejudice and conflict were increased tremendously by the development of the slave trade. In turn, the industrial revolution contributed enormously to the wealth and prestige of the white people of Europe and America. Darwin's doctrine of evolution, with the idea of the survival of the fittest, "was warmly accepted by the people of European stock who saw no reason to doubt that they were the fittest of all." [19]

Whatever the source of contemporary racial prejudice, it has become practically universal. It may help us to make a wiser approach to the situation if we recognize that all racial groups are prejudiced, at least to some degree. The reasons for their prejudices and the expression of them may differ, but none is entirely free from prejudice.

A first step in handling our prejudices is to understand why we have them. Although some racial prejudice seems to be almost universal, the students of prejudice generally

---

[18] Arnold J. Toynbee, *A Study of History* (2d ed.; London: Oxford University Press, 1935), I, 223.

[19] Alan Burns, *Colour Prejudice* (London: George Allen and Unwin Ltd., 1948), p. 23.

would agree with Montagu that no animal or human is born with any fear or prejudice but that these are acquired or learned. This does not necessarily mean that there is no instinctive basis for racial prejudice. It seems that there is, to some degree, an innate aversion for an individual who is noticeably different from the accepted norm for the group. Most people shrink away from the crippled, the deformed, the queer, even of their own race. The child, however, does not seem to be as conscious of such differences as older people. The consciousness of others reaches its peak with the adolescent when the individual becomes most aware of himself as a distinct personality and hence most conscious of other personalities. This consciousness of self, of one's group, and of others and their differences does not necessarily lead to racial prejudice and antagonism. Racial prejudice, at least primarily, comes from some other source or sources.

One of the main sources for racial prejudice is the social heritage. Prejudice is an integral phase of that heritage for most children. In other words, a person catches his prejudices very much like he catches the measles. He lives in an environment where the contagion runs high. Racial prejudices are very infectious or easily communicable. It would be a miracle if the individual did not contract the disease.

Racial prejudice is heightened by economic and social competition. Usually the larger the minority group, the greater is the economic competition and the stronger and more vocal becomes the prejudice. That explains, to a considerable degree, the strength of the prejudice against the Negro in the South, the Mexican in the Southwest, and the Japanese on the Pacific Coast. As increasing numbers of Negroes have moved to the urban centers of the North, racial tension and feeling have increased in those areas.

Regardless of what may be the source of racial prejudice —which may be defined as a tendency to evaluate an individual primarily on the basis of his identity with a group thought of as racial—its effects are bad. It is what Pearl Buck calls "the dark shadow"—a shadow not only over the Negro and other minority racial groups but over all of us and possibly darkest over those who feel it least. It is like a "cancer in the heart of human society." [20] If we let our prejudices control us, we tend to act without thinking. This is always bad. Under the compulsion of prejudice we tend to identify individuals with racial groups rather than with the human race. Surely we will agree that when we act on the basis of prejudice, we are not being as Christian as we should be. Giving expression to our prejudices is a sign of intellectual and spiritual immaturity.

The effects of prejudice are also bad on the victim. They tend to create in him a sense of inferiority, of defeatism, or of resentment and a determination to get even. Those of us who belong to the majority "we" group cannot possibly know fully the reactions of minority peoples to racial prejudice. This is even true of those who keep their emotions under strict control. A well-educated, cultured, mature Christian Negro, in speaking to a group of white students, quietly said, "You white young people do not know what segregation, which is a product of prejudice, means." Then he added very impressively, but without bitterness, "I know what it means. I have experienced it in my own life." This man was a high school principal with an advanced degree from one of the leading American universities, and with a daughter at that time working on an M.A. degree in an Eastern university. His statement that day will linger in the minds of those white students as long as they live.

The effects of racial prejudice are adverse not only on the ones having the prejudice and the victims of that prejudice but also upon the community. Although the South has made remarkable progress in many ways, it has not measured up to its great potential. One reason for its failure to advance as

[20] Henry Smith Leiper, *Blind Spots* (rev. ed.; New York: Friendship Press, 1944), p. xi.

rapidly as it should has been its treatment of the Negro. This reminds us of the familiar statement attributed to Booker T. Washington that you cannot hold a man down in a ditch without staying down there with him. If the Southern states want to lift themselves, they in some way must lift the status of the Negro, their largest "you" group.

It is also true that any mistreatment of Negro and other minority groups is a major handicap to the United States in its attempt to provide moral leadership for the world. Communism has taken advantage, at every point possible, of our failure to apply fully our democratic principles to minority groups. Racial prejudice, particularly in its practical expression, is also a very real handicap to the cause of Christian missions. As Christians we should consider seriously the effects of racial prejudice on us, on others, on our nation, and on the cause of Christ in our local communities and out to the ends of the earth.

V

"LOVE YOUR NEIGHBOR"

And a second is like it, You shall love your neigh-
bor as yourself.   MATTHEW 22:39

An understanding of the context of a statement will give a better basis for a correct interpretation and evaluation of it. This certainly is true of the great statement of Jesus, from which the preceding is taken. The words "love your neighbor" were spoken by Jesus in response to a question by a scribe (see Mark 12:28), who was identified as a lawyer ("an expert in the law," Phillips; "an expounder of the Law," Weymouth), and who was a spokesman for a group of Pharisees. Some of the scribes who had become recognized not only as authoritative copyists of the Law but also as interpreters of it were called lawyers.

The Pharisees had heard that Jesus had silenced (literally, "muzzled") the Sadducees. The former doubtless received this report with real satisfaction, since the Sadducees were their traditional rivals and enemies and since the resurrection, which was the point at which Jesus had silenced the Sadducees, was a favorite and distinctive doctrine of the Pharisees.

The Pharisees came together, obviously to pool their thinking concerning some question they might ask Jesus. The question the lawyer, as their spokesman, asked frequently was debated by the scribes and Pharisees. They argued about which were the weightier and more important and the lighter and less significant of the Commandments. They asked Jesus for his judgment. They did this to test or to tempt him. This could mean that the lawyer was trying to get Jesus into a corner. On the other hand, it could merely mean that he was testing Jesus' knowledge and discernment of the Law and was curious to know what his reply would be. As Robertson suggests, Jesus cut through the scribal "pettifogging hair-splitting to the heart of the problem." [1]

Love for God and Man

The lawyer's question was, "Teacher, which is the great commandment in the law?" ("what sort of command is greatest in the law?" Williams). The question seems not to have been so much about a particular commandment as it was "about the qualities that determine greatness in the legal region." [2] What kind or type was greatest? Jesus answered that it was a commandment of love. Quoting Deuteronomy 6:5, he said, "You shall love the Lord your God with all your heart, and with all your soul, and with all your mind." Following the quotation Jesus added: "This is the great and first commandment" ("this is the greatest command, and is first in importance," Williams). Here is stated man's supreme responsibility and privilege. Let us never forget that the greatest commandment "in dignity, in excellence, in extent, and duration," which is "the fountain of all others," [3] is love for God and that we are to love him with our total personalities.

Love for God is first, but there is a second command like it. Why did Jesus, after giving the greatest and first commandment, add, possibly after a deliberate pause, "And a second is like it, You shall love your neighbor as yourself"? The lawyer had asked for only *the* great commandment. Why should Jesus give the second, which he quoted from Leviticus 19:18? It might have been that he recognized that the Pharisees particularly needed the second. Or it might have been

[1] Robertson, *op. cit.*, I, 177.

[2] A. B. Bruce, *The Synoptic Gospels* (*The Expositor's Greek Testament,* ed. W. Robertson Nicoll [Grand Rapids: Wm. B. Eerdmans Publishing Co., n.d.]), I, 276.

[3] Albert Barnes, *Matthew-Mark* (*Notes on the New Testament* [New York: Harper & Brothers, n.d.]), I, 237.

that here "Jesus not only penetrated and convicted the wicked design of the Pharisees, but also reproved the error that lurked in their question." [4] If he was doing the latter, he was correcting an error that persists even in our day. There are still many, similar to the Pharisees of the days of Jesus, who believe that they can love God and hate their fellow man, that they can be right with God and wrong with those who have been created in the image of God. Jesus is saying here that love for God and love for man cannot be separated; they belong together.

What did Jesus mean when he said that the second was like the first? Possibly he meant that it also was a command of love. It is also possible, as suggested previously, that he was saying to his day and to our day that the second is like unto the first in importance. One is incomplete without the other.

According to Mark's record, after Jesus stated these two commandments, he added, "There is no other commandment greater than these" (Mark 12:31). Notice the singular, "There *is* no other commandment." It may be that by using the singular Jesus meant to say "that duty, like God, was one, in opposition to the prevailing habit of viewing duty as consisting in isolated precepts." [5] But there is also the possibility that here again Jesus was suggesting that these two commandments are so closely related that they can be considered as one. [6]

Few, if any, of the Jews who heard Jesus give the great summary of the Law would or even could object to the commandments he quoted. These two were used by some of the Jewish teachers and scholars to sum up the requirements of

---

[4] Johann Peter Lange, "Matthew," *Commentary on the Holy Scriptures,* trans. Phillip Schaaf (Grand Rapids: Zondervan Publishing House, 1949–51), p. 404.

[5] Bruce, *op. cit.,* p. 424.

[6] A careful reading of 1 John, giving particular attention to love of God and love of fellow man and their interrelatedness, could be a very rewarding experience for any one.

the Law. This may be the explanation for the summary by the lawyer in Luke's account (10:25–28), which provided a portion of the background for the parable of the good Samaritan.

Limits of Love

Luke says that a lawyer ("an expert in the law," Williams) stood up to put Jesus to the test, saying, "Teacher, what shall I do to inherit eternal life?" Jesus in turn asked, "What is written in the law? How do you read?" The lawyer then quoted Deuteronomy 6:5 and Leviticus 19:18. Jesus then said to him, "You have answered right; do this, and you will live." Jesus here uses a verb form which carries the idea of continuous action. What he said was "keep on doing this and you shall live." This made love something that was deeper and more meaningful than the lawyer had realized.

No wonder the lawyer, whose conscience was possibly half-awakened and uneasy, should ask, "And who is my neighbor?" The fact that he inquired about his neighbor implies that Jesus had touched a tender spot in his life when he said, "Keep on loving your neighbor as yourself, and you shall live."

The lawyer, wishing to find some basis on which he could justify himself, inquired about the breadth of love. He seemed to say: "Admitting that I am to love my neighbor as myself, whom am I to consider my neighbor? There must be some limits to neighbor and hence to love." Do we tend to ask similar questions? Do we tend to set limits for "neighbor"? Do we seek to limit love?

Even if we legitimately could limit "neighbor" to fellow Christians and hence limit our obligation to love, would this by any stretch of the imagination justify any class or racial limitations? All who know Christ as Saviour are our brothers in Christ. Whatever interpretation we may place on "neighbor," we cannot find any justifiable basis for color consciousness in the area of Christian love. Jesus did not say, "Love

71

your white neighbor or your colored neighbor," but rather, "Love your neighbor."

Furthermore, there are many specific teachings in the Bible that plainly say that love should go beyond the Christian circle. In Peter's great list of the Christian virtues "brotherly affection" is followed by "love," which is the climax of all (2 Peter 1:5-7). Paul in writing to the Thessalonians said, "And may the Lord make you increase and abound in love to one another and to all men, as we do to you" (1 Thess. 3:12). Notice here the uniting of "one another" and "all men." We cannot love God as we should without loving one another, and we cannot love God supremely and one another as we should without loving all men; and "all men" is broad, just as "love" is deep as well as broad.

Let us repeat that the lawyer wanted Jesus to place some limits on "neighbor." He wanted "his moral duties to be labelled and defined with the Talmudic precision to which ceremonial duties had been reduced." [7] Generally speaking, the Jews split hairs over the definition of neighbor and they "excluded from 'neighbour' Gentiles and especially Samaritans," [8] but Jesus never placed limits on his basic teachings. They were, and are, all limitless. They could not be otherwise and be ideals of perfection. And unless they were ideals of perfection, they would not be constantly challenging and hence abidingly relevant.

Jesus did not answer the lawyer's question directly, although his question was answered, in one sense, in a very radical way. Jesus by implication said that any man who is in need is a neighbor. That was radical for that day and even for our day.

By means of the story of the good Samaritan, which incidentally is found only in Luke, Jesus answered more specifically a far more important question than the one the lawyer asked. The lawyer had asked, "Who is my neighbor?" At the

[7] Farrar, op. cit., p. 204.
[8] Robertson, op. cit., II, 152.

conclusion of the story of the good Samaritan, Jesus asked the lawyer the searching question, "Which of these three, do you think, proved neighbor to the man who fell among the robbers?" The more important question that Jesus answered was, "How can I be a good neighbor?" This is far more important for us, as it was for the lawyer, than, "Who is my neighbor?" What a contrast between the lawyer, who had asked the less important question, and the Samaritan, who by his conduct answered the more important question! The latter, rather than "seeking limits to his love, freely and largely exercised it towards one whose only claim upon him consisted in his needs." [9]

In the conversation of Jesus with the lawyer we see the Master Teacher at work. The wise teacher leads those whom he teaches to discover truth for themselves. The fact that the lawyer was led to answer the question Jesus asked undoubtedly made a deeper and more lasting impression on him than any statement Jesus could have made.

Notice the answer of the lawyer to the probing question by Jesus. Jesus asked him, "Which one of the three was a neighbor unto the one who fell among the robbers?" The lawyer's reply was, "The one who showed mercy on him." Burton says that he replied "with no hesitation, but with a lingering prejudice that does not care to pronounce the, to him, outlandish name." [10] Robertson says, "He gulped at the word 'Samaritan.'" [11]

Jesus then said to him, "Go and do likewise." What had the Samaritan done? He had proved his love for a fellow human being by caring for him in a time of need. The thing that made his actions stand out more clearly was the fact that his kindness was "from a 'despised schismatic,' overcoming

[9] R. C. Trench, *Notes on the Parables of Our Lord* (New York: Fleming H. Revell, n.d.), p. 252.

[10] Henry Burton, *The Gospel According to St. Luke* (*The Expositor's Bible*, ed. W. Robertson Nicoll [Grand Rapids: Wm. B. Eerdmans Publishing Co., 1940]), V, 83.

[11] *Op. cit.*, II, 155.

racial ill-feeling though it could expect no similar kindness in return." [12] Would the lawyer, a Jew, have been as generous to the Samaritan under similar circumstances? The preceding properly implies that the parable is really an amplification of the Golden Rule. This is suggested in the original statement of the principle, "Love your neighbor as yourself."

The parable of the good Samaritan also emphasizes that neighbor and neighborly are coextensive with humanity. Men may magnify their differences. They may pride themselves upon them, "but how little does Heaven make of them! Heaven does not even see them. Our national boundaries [and we might add "our racial boundaries"] may climb up over the Alps, but they cannot touch the sky. Those skies look down and smile on all alike." [13] Again the same author graphically says, "In the mind of Jesus, as in the purpose of God, humanity was not a group of fractions, but a unit one and indivisible, made of one blood, and by one Blood redeemed." [14] Robertson sums up the impact of this parable as follows: "This parable of the Good Samaritan has built the world's hospitals and, if understood and practised, will remove race prejudice, national hatred and war, class jealousy." [15] Let us all pray that the peoples of the world, even the Christian peoples of the world, may soon understand and practice the Golden Rule of the parable of the good Samaritan.

This section on the limits of love would not be complete without at least a brief statement concerning the teachings of Jesus regarding love for one's enemies. This is involved, to some degree, in the story of the good Samaritan. The Jews considered the Samaritans their enemies. It is possible that Jesus had in mind this current Jewish attitude when he said in the Sermon on the Mount, "You have heard that it was

[12] Luce, *op. cit.*, p. 116.
[13] Burton, *op. cit.*, p. 83.
[14] *Ibid.*, p. 83.
[15] *Op. cit.*, II, 155.

said, 'You shall love your neighbor and hate your enemy.' "
In contrast, Jesus made love all-inclusive when he said, "But
I say to you, Love your enemies and pray for those who persecute you" (Matt. 5:43–44). We show our kinship to our
Heavenly Father by loving without limits. As his children
we aspire, or should aspire, to be like him. If we love only
those who love us, what do we more than the peoples of the
world? They respond to the love of others. Such response is
natural. We are to live above the natural level. Jesus' call to
us as his disciples is not "to be moral mediocrities, men of
average morality, but to be morally superior, uncommon." [16]
Nothing less is worthy of our Lord.

One of the most adequate and accurate ways to measure
our kinship to God is the breadth, depth, and genuineness of
our love. Love is the very essence of his being. He loves all
men. His blessings are showered upon the evil and the good,
upon the unjust and the just. Is our love close enough akin to
his that it reaches out in active good will to all men regardless of race, class, or condition of life?

As we shall see later, Christian love is more than a super-
ficial sentiment. But the question abidingly remains to challenge and search us: Do we love all men, even our enemies?
If we do, it will be natural for us to love in a special way
those who are our brothers in Christ, who are children of our
Heavenly Father. This will be true of all of them, regardless
of their color. Surely Christian love can and will find a way
to express itself in these days of racial conflict and strife. Let
us hope and pray that the love of God, which rests upon
and abides within us, will enable us to maintain Christian
fellowship across racial lines in the midst of mounting tension. May Christians everywhere, in the spirit of supreme
love for God and genuine love for their fellow man, join
hearts, heads, and hands in discovering solutions for the perplexing problems of our day.

[16] Bruce, *op. cit.*, p. 115.

Love and the Law

Following Jesus' citation of "the great and first commandment" and the second that was like unto it are the following words: "On these two commandments depend all the law and the prophets" (Matt. 22:40). The key word in this statement is "depend." It means to hang or suspend. "The figure is taken from the door on its hinges, or from the nail on the wall," [17] or a peg on which garments are hung.

What did Jesus mean when he said that the Law and the Prophets are suspended or hung on these two commandments? We are not sure that we know the depth of his meaning, but evidently he meant that all the precepts of the Old Testament Scriptures were fulfilled in, and included under, one of these commandments of love. These commandments lie at the root of all the requirements and represent the moral drift of the entire Old Testament. Weymouth and Williams both have caught something of this idea in their translations. Weymouth says, "The whole of the Law and the Prophets is summed up in these two Commandments." Williams expresses the same general idea, but more graphically, when he says, "The essence of the whole law and the prophets is packed into these two commands." Notice the words "summed up" and "packed into."

Let us consider the relation of these commandments to the moral law of the Old Testament. The basic requirements of that moral law are summarized in the two tables of the Law, the Ten Commandments. The first table of the Law had to do with man's relations or duties to God. The second table deals with man's relations to his fellow man. The two commandments given by Jesus clearly comprehend the substance of all that was in both of these tables which, to repeat, represented a summary of the fundamental moral law. If one loves God supremely, he will keep the first table of the Law: he will not have any other God than the true God;

[17] Lange, *op. cit.*, p. 404.

he will not make any graven image; he will not take the name of the Lord God in vain; and he will remember the sabbath day to keep it holy. On the other hand, if one loves his neighbor as himself, he will observe the requirements of the second table: he will honor his father and mother; he will not kill; he will not commit adultery; he will not steal; he will not bear false witness; and he will not covet. Jesus specifically related "you shall love your neighbor" to the second table in his conversation with the rich young ruler (Matt. 19:16–22).

Jesus' summary of the Law under the two commandments of love must have become an integral and an important part of the oral tradition and later of the written record of his teachings. We find it specifically referred to on more than one occasion by Paul. For example, after his instructions concerning the relation of Christians to "the powers that be" he says, "Owe no one anything, except to love one another," and then adds, "For he who loves his neighbor has fulfilled the law." He follows this statement with a quotation of some of the Ten Commandments from the second table and says that these "and any other commandment, are summed up in this sentence, 'You shall love your neighbor as yourself.'" He then gives the reason why this is true: "Love does no wrong to a neighbor; therefore love is the fulfilling of the law" (see Rom. 13:8–10). The way Paul relates these verses to the preceding section on the Christian's relation to government or the powers that be seems to suggest that he is saying, "When you have paid all your other debts, taxes, and customs, and reverence, and whatever else you may owe, there will still be one debt unpaid—the universal debt of love."[18] Robertson says, "This debt can never be paid off, but we should keep the interest paid up."[19]

Paul also admonished the Galatian Christians "through

---

[18] W. Sanday, *The Epistle to the Romans* in *A Bible Commentary for Bible Students,* ed. C. J. Ellicott, VII, 257.

[19] *Op. cit.,* IV, 409.

love" to be "servants of one another." He then said, "For the whole law is fulfilled in one word, 'You shall love your neighbor as yourself'" (Gal. 5:13–14). No wonder James designates love of neighbor as "the royal law" (James 2:8). Let us not forget that James applies this royal law to partiality or respect of persons in the church. If we are respecters of persons, if we show partiality, we have violated the fundamental command to love our neighbors as ourselves.

Some people tend to brush aside Christian love as too idealistic. Some even say that it cannot be applied in an evil world. They suggest that the best we can do is to achieve equal justice or relative love. When properly understood, it will be seen that Christian love, as is true of other standards of the Christian message, is very idealistic. But there is no full achievement of Christian ends without the use of Christian methods; and certainly love and the love ethic have an important place in any Christian approach to human problems. Robertson says that "love is the only solution of our social relations and national problems." [20] One of our major social and national issues is the race problem.

The Language of Love

What is the language of love? There are some things it is not. It does not speak the language of hate. It will not join with those extremists who would stir up racial animosity. It will not designate people by undignified and odious names. Love will not use ostracism, economic boycott, or social pressure to attempt to force people to conform to a prescribed code or pattern. Love will not appeal to prejudice. It will not appeal to the baser human emotions. On the other hand, it will not be blind to the difficulties it faces. It will be intelligent rather than emotional in its approach to the problems of life, including those related to the race issue.

The love we are talking about, and have been talking about throughout this chapter, is a special kind of love or a

[20] *Ibid.*

love with a special quality. It is not human love, at least not in the ordinary sense. It is a love that partakes of the divine quality. It is expressed by *agape*, a Greek word that is very prevalent in the New Testament. The word is so distinctive in its meaning and so different from the generally accepted modern conception of love that some New Testament scholars contend that it should not have been translated but merely transliterated, and hence it would have become a word in our language.

Agape gives itself to the object loved. Its language is self-denial and self-sacrifice. It says: "God so loved the world that he gave . . ." (John 3:16); "Christ loved the church and gave himself up for her" (Eph. 5:25); "Greater love has no man than this, that a man lay down his life for his friends" (John 15:13). Notice the verse immediately preceding the last one quoted. Jesus had said, "This is my commandment, that you love one another as I have loved you." How had he loved them? Enough that he was going to give his life for them and for us. Following this he suggests that they should love one another enough to lay down their lives. These and many other verses in the Bible speak the language of *agape*.

Agape is also spontaneous and unmotivated, at least unmotivated by anything outside of itself. In a sense it is "a lost love," a love extended to those who do not return it, or at least they may not return it. It is never selfish but always unselfish. To use Buber's definition in his typical terminology, "Love is responsibility of an *I* for a *Thou*." [21] And incidentally, *agape*, or Christian love, treats another person primarily as a "thou" and not as an "it."

What is the source of this type or quality of love? It is the Christian's union with God through his faith in Christ. "Christian love is the highest expression of the unity of the soul with God." By faith we come into union with him and he with us. We surrender to him, we submit ourselves to

[21] Martin Buber, *I and Thou*, trans. Ronald Gregor Smith (New York: Charles Scribner's Sons, 1937), p. 15.

him. "Through love we rise up to fellowship with him. . . . Faith makes us receptive to the spirit of God; love makes the spirit of God operative in us." Another way of saying the same thing is to say that "Christian love is the love of God operating in the human heart." [22] Here is our chief hope for improved human relations.

The "spirit" in the above could properly be capitalized. It is Paul who says that "the fruit of the Spirit is love, joy, peace, patience, kindness, goodness, faithfulness, gentleness, self-control; against such there is no law" (Gal. 5:22-23). Notice that "fruit" is singular, suggesting unity, in contrast to the "works of the flesh" (v. 19). There is a sense in which all of the fruit of the Spirit is grounded in love. Love is first; it is basic; the others evolve from it. It is love that "binds everything together in perfect harmony" (Col. 3:14).

What about laying our lives down beside God's standard of excellence, as revealed in these verses from Galatians? Do we have the fruit of the Spirit? Do we express the fruit of the Spirit in our relations to those of other racial groups? For example, are we patient, kind, and gentle in our dealings with them? Does *agape* find expression within us and hence through us in our relations with them?

A biracial group was discussing human relations. One phase of the discussion was an emphasis on Christian love as a factor in good relations with those of one's own race and with those of other races. A cultured, refined Negro college teacher, a Ph.D. from a leading American university, raised the following searching questions: "Is there not some danger that love will become a shallow sentimentality? Do not many people substitute love for justice? Is it not true that some people who claim to love the Negro at the same time justify and defend the injustices he suffers under the generally accepted racial pattern?"

These questions do suggest some real dangers. They represent pitfalls into which some people are falling and against

[22] Unpublished address by George D. Kelsey.

which all of us should guard. However, when anyone makes love an idle, empty sentimentality or substitutes it for justice, he has a very limited, inadequate, and distorted conception of Christian love. His idea of love is not *agape*. *Agape* knows nothing of love without justice. Justice, in the most meaningful way, is a derivative of *agape*. Love with the *agape* quality transcends justice. It can only do more and never less than justice demands. "Only when love is in the heart can justice be established in the world." [23]

Justice and love belong together. They cannot be separated because they are united in God. God is a God both of love and of justice. Both qualities should be maintained in proper balance in our lives. Justice can check and punish evil; love alone can overcome and redeem evil. Love expresses itself in justice. On the other hand, justice is to be kept under the constant scrutiny of Christian love.

Tillich defines love as "the drive towards the unity of the separated," as "the reunion of the estranged." [24] This is *agape*, this is divine love. It is true of God's love for man. His love for man is "the drive towards the unity of the separated" (God and man are separated), toward "the reunion of the estranged" (man is estranged from God). The same is true in human relations. Real Christian love, love that partakes of the *agape* quality, is an urge, a tug, a drive toward the uniting of those who are separated, who are estranged from each other. Think of what a contribution such love could make to the easing of the contemporary racial tensions, to the solution of perplexing racial and human problems!

How much does the spirit of *agape* possess us and express itself through us in our relations with others? Let us quietly, prayerfully re-examine our lives in the light of Paul's great

[23] William Temple, *Thoughts in War-Time* (London: Macmillan and Co. Ltd., 1940), p. 29.

[24] Paul Tillich, *Love, Power, and Justice* (New York: Oxford University Press, 1954), p. 25.

love chapter. He says: "Love is patient and kind; love is not jealous or boastful; it is not arrogant or rude. Love does not insist on its own way; it is not irritable or resentful; it does not rejoice at wrong, but rejoices in the right. Love bears all things, believes all things, hopes all things, endures all things" (1 Cor. 13:4–7).

Sometimes we think only of the portions of these and the other verses of the chapter that might apply to the underprivileged or to the persecuted. All of it, if rightly understood, applies to each of us, the privileged as well as the underprivileged. Some of it, however, in a particular way applies to those who belong to the majority or "we" group. Take the time to read prayerfully and to meditate upon the message of 1 Corinthians 13. Let its message grip your heart and its spirit permeate your life. If you will, it will be a great blessing to you and will make you a greater blessing to others.

When we think of the blessings that have come to us and our world through *agape*, Christian love, we do not wonder that Paul introduces the great love chapter with, "I will show you a still more excellent way," and ends it with the immortal words: "So faith, hope, love abide, these three; but the greatest of these is love."

VI

"TEACHING THEM"

Go therefore and make disciples of all nations,
baptizing them in the name of the Father and of the
Son and of the Holy Spirit, teaching them to observe
all that I have commanded you; and lo, I am with
you always, to the close of the age.

MATTHEW 28:19–20

The preceding is Matthew's record of the Commission of our Lord, which was given to his disciples at the climax of his post-resurrection appearance. When properly understood, we find in it sufficient authority for everything that Christians and their churches should do. It is a composite of theology, evangelism, Christian ethics, religious education, and Christian symbolism. It includes the assurance of the presence and, by implication, the glorious return of the resurrected Christ.

As we study the Commission, we shall seek to interpret it in general, but we shall also call attention to its relation to the contemporary racial situation.

"Go Therefore"

What was the background for the "therefore"? It was the statement Jesus had just made that all authority in heaven and on earth had been given to him. The "in heaven and on earth" would be inclusive of all authority. Here is the background for his sending his disciples and also for their responding to his command to go. They could go with the certainty that all power or authority had been given to the One who gave the command to go. He had the authority to order them to go, but also when they went, they could go with the assurance that the authority and power that was his would surround, support, and strengthen them.

This authority had been *given* to him. The verb form suggests that it had been given to him at a specific time in the past. However, that which had been given to him he still possessed. Whether given at the time of his resurrection or merely authenticated at that time is immaterial. We know that when he stood before his disciples that day, he had all authority, and that authority was not and is not delegated to his disciples. "It remains, and must remain with Him. . . . They must keep in closest touch with Him, wherever they go," [1] if they are to have that power.

The "on earth" part of the statement by Jesus has important implications in the whole area of applied Christianity. It reminds us of the petition in the prayer which he taught his disciples:

> Thy kingdom come,
> thy will be done,
>   on earth as it is in heaven (Matt. 6:10).

His will is done perfectly in heaven; his purpose is that his will should be done perfectly on earth. To this end his disciples should pray and work.

Christ is not concerned exclusively with any one segment of life. He has authority in every realm, and he wants that authority to be realized and recognized. He would say to his disciples today as he did then, "Go and make that power a reality in every area of life." What a limited conception of the authority and the concern of Christ a person must have who would say, as one was heard to say recently, "I do not see how being a Christian has anything to do with the race problem." Such a statement does not fit in with "all authority . . . on earth."

---

[1] John Monro Gibson, *The Gospel of St. Matthew* (*The Expositor's Bible* [Grand Rapids: Wm. B. Eerdmans Publishing Co., 1940]), IV, 809.

"Make Disciples"

There is a need for a verb "to disciple" in the English language. The best possible translation, under the limitations of our language, is "make disciples." This is the initial emphasis in the Commission that Jesus gave to his disciples. It is basic. Everything else we do for him depends on it. However, it should be remembered that this phase of the Commission, as important as it is, is only one purpose in a comprehensive commission. Winning others to Christ, enrolling them in his school as learners, is the absolutely necessary first step. But it is the first and not the final step.

As we seek to win or to enlist others, we should remember that we ourselves are disciples. Those who are disciples are the only ones who can win others to discipleship. But what does it mean to be a disciple? We know that Jesus, from the early days of his ministry, called some of those who followed him "disciples." For example, when he taught the wonderful lessons that we designate as the Sermon on the Mount, he called his disciples to him and taught them. This suggests that the disciples were pupils, or learners. The word "disciple" was used rather generally in this sense. The Pharisees had their disciples (Matt. 22:16), and John the Baptist had his (Matt. 9:14; 11:2; 14:12).

There are some places where the word "disciple" as used by Jesus referred to those who not only listened to his words and hence were learners but who also believed and submitted "themselves to his authority as a teacher." [2] A disciple in the truest and deepest sense accepts the yoke of authoritative instruction, believes what the teacher says is true because he says it, and submits to the teacher's requirements as right simply because he makes them.

The term "yoke" was used to express the relation of a pupil to his teacher. The rabbis spoke of the yoke of the

[2] John A. Broadus, *Commentary on the Gospel of Matthew* (*An American Commentary on the New Testament*, ed. Alvah Hovey [Philadelphia: American Baptist Publication Society, n.d.]), I, 87.

Law. Jesus, when he used the term "yoke," utilized a common term, but frequently he injected new meaning and depth into it. His yoke would be easy, his burden light. However,

Only the man who follows the command of Jesus without reserve, and submits unresistingly to His yoke, finds His burden easy. . . . The command of Jesus is hard, unutterably hard, for those who try to resist it. But for those who willingly submit, the yoke is easy, and the burden is light.[3]

As we seek to enlist others in the school of Christ, as we try to get them to accept the yoke he offers to them, we should remember that we ourselves are his disciples, that we have taken his yoke upon us. We are students in the school of Christ. We, along with those whom we enlist, need to sit at his feet and learn of him. This is as true of the most mature as it is of the least mature. We all need to be instructed by him. As we mature, the instruction can and should be on a higher level. We should be progressively better prepared to digest solid food or the strong meat of the Word (1 Cor. 3:2; Heb. 5:12–14). To be very personal, have you and I progressed in the school of Christ to the place where we are mature in our attitudes toward persons of other races and classes? There are many Christians who in most ways seem to be quite mature but who are infantile in their general racial attitudes. They react to contemporary racial problems and tensions as children and not as adults. They are driven largely by emotion and controlled by prejudice rather than by sound judgment based on Christian principles.

One evidence of a mature Christian is that he has worked out within his own mind and soul, under the guidance of the indwelling Spirit, what he considers to be right. His conception of right is based on what he interprets to be the will of God. It is not necessarily derived from, nor can it be

[3] Dietrich Bonhoeffer, *The Cost of Discipleship,* trans. R. H. Fuller (London: SCM Press, 1948), p. 31.

equated with, public opinion. Knowing what he considers to be right, the mature child of God will do and defend that. He will not drift with the crowd. His attitude and his action will not depend on where he is and what the prevailing attitude is.

Again, how mature are we regarding the racial situation? Do we approach it objectively, or do we emotionalize the whole situation? Do we control our prejudices, or are we controlled by them? Are we swayed by mass opinion, or do we seek to apply the Christian spirit and ideals to the problem? What is our level of living in the area of race relations? Are we still in the kindergarten or the elementary school when we should be on the high school, college, or university level?

"Of All Nations"

The "all nations" of the Commission suggests its geographic, national, and racial inclusiveness. As his disciples go with the gospel, they are not to be respecters of persons. They are to go as readily to one racial, national, or class group as to another. This portion of the Commission, as is true of the Commission as a whole, reveals the essential missionary nature of the Christian movement. "It must spread, by a law of its nature; it must be active at the extremities, or it becomes chilled at the heart; must be enlarging its circumference, or its very centre tends to be defaced."[4]

To be true to its nature the Christian religion must not only be active at geographic extremities but it must also be active at what some consider to be moral and social extremities. Just as it cannot be true to its genius and establish any boundaries for its missionary endeavor, likewise, it cannot be true to its genius and set any boundaries for the application of its spirit and principles. To do the latter would tend to rob it of its vitality.

[4] Broadus, *op. cit.*, p. 593.

"Teaching Them to Observe"

The teaching element is very prominent in the Great Commission. As suggested previously, the disciple was a pupil or learner. Winning individuals to Christ as Saviour and Lord implies enlisting them in a learning process. An important element in the learning process is what the pupil learns from association with the teacher. He learns from what the teacher is as well as from what he says. Great teachers are always such, not only in their teaching methods, but also in their spirit. Jesus was and is the world's greatest teacher.

Those who have been won to Christ are to be baptized in the name of the Father, Son, and Holy Spirit. In baptism they put on the uniform of the Christian movement. They definitely identify themselves as disciples of Christ. Baptism is one of the first steps they take in obedience to the Master Teacher, who is the Lord of their lives. The ordinance itself in a very real way is a teaching method. By visual method it teaches the death, burial, and resurrection of Christ. It also testifies to others that the one who is baptized has died to the old life and has been raised to walk in newness of life. In a sense it is, in picture form, a committal of life to the lordship of Christ.

The fact that "teaching them" comes after "discipling" and "baptizing" does not mean that teaching is to be restricted to the postbaptismal period. As previously implied, a certain amount of teaching can properly, and must inevitably, precede the enrolling of the individual in the school of Christ. He has to know something about Christ before he can accept him as Saviour and Lord.

Although teaching performs an important function before conversion, it fills a much more significant place after conversion and baptism. There is a very real sense in which the individual cannot understand the great truths that Christ taught until he has come into union with Christ. The deeper things of the Spirit can be grasped only by those who walk in the Spirit. But even those who are children of God and are seeking as best they can to walk in, or under the guiding impulse of, the Spirit need to be taught. They do not inevitably and automatically understand the great truths of Christ.

This means that the making and baptizing of disciples is not our total task. "The person who is discipled and baptized is only started in a course of Christian living."[5] It is our business to see that he makes progress in that course, while at the same time we should be sure that we ourselves are making progress.

The "all that I have commanded you" suggests the content of the teaching. What did and does it include? The answer to this question is found, in the main, in the Gospels. We may properly believe, however, that "all that I have commanded you" also includes "much unrecorded teaching which they had heard in the darkness, and were to reproduce in light (chap. x. 27)."[6] The recorded material alone, however, is enough to challenge us to the end of life's journey.

If you want a real blessing in your life, read carefully and prayerfully one of the Gospels, preferably Matthew, asking the Holy Spirit to be your teacher. Underscore or make a list of the things Jesus taught. Give special consideration to their relation to human problems in general and to the contemporary racial situation in particular. It is important to remember that the teachings of Jesus are abidingly relevant. They stand in constant judgment against our imperfect approximation of them in our lives and in our society.

Could what Jesus said to the Pharisees and scribes on one occasion apply to many people today? He said to them, "You leave the commandment of God, and hold fast the tradition of men." He repeated his charge even more plainly

[5] *Ibid.*, p. 596.
[6] *Ellicott's Commentary*, VI, 183.

THE BIBLE AND RACE

by saying, "You have a fine way of rejecting the commandment of God, in order to keep your tradition!" (Mark 7:8–9).
Are some people today rejecting some of the commandments
of Jesus in order to hold on to certain racial traditions? The
supreme question for these days is not what has been or are
the traditions of the South or of any other regions but rather,
what is the will of God? The test of conduct should not be
what others think but what God commands.

We should not only do what Christ commands; we should
also teach others to obey his commands. Teaching is an important phase of the Christian social application. There are
some methods of social change, such as the political or legislative, that may be used with discretion by Christians. There
are other methods that form an integral part of the Christian
approach to social and moral reform. Education belongs
within the latter category. It, along with conversion or
regeneration and demonstration, represents the distinctly
Christian approach.

Most of us recognize the importance of bringing men into
a vital life-changing union with God through faith in Christ.
We correctly believe that the disciple's first and supreme
task is to make other disciples. It is unfortunate, however,
that many who believe this most strongly fail to appreciate
the importance of the teaching function. They do not seem
to realize that the born-again individual does not and cannot naturally know fully what it means to follow Christ. He
will not inevitably express the spirit of Christ in his relations
with others. He is a babe in Christ. He needs to be nur-
tured, taught, and trained. He cannot comprehend all the
implications of this new experience he has had with Christ
unless someone instructs him. "Regeneration merely creates
the will to do the right; it does not define for a man what is
right." [7] The definition of what is right is one purpose of
Christian education.

[7] Walter Rauschenbusch, *Christianity and the Social Crisis* (New York:
Hodder & Stoughton, 1907), p. 354.

Let us return for a moment to the teaching emphasis in the Great Commission. Notice that the resurrected Christ did not merely say, "Teaching them all that I have commanded you," but rather, "Teaching them *to observe* all . . ." The expression "to observe" is translated "to practice" by Williams. It is a big and an important task to teach those who have been won to Christ to know what he taught or commanded. It is even a bigger and more difficult task to lead them to obey or practice what they know. This involves the exercise of the will, the quality which makes us most distinctly men. There is a sense in which a man does not really know a thing until he has obeyed it. When he obeys the truth that he knows theoretically or intellectually, then he knows it actually or experientially.

At least one purpose of Jesus in the Commission was that those who had been "discipled" might be led to live a life worthy of their divine vocation. "The teaching is with a view not to *gnosis* but to practice; the aim not orthodox opinion but right living." [8] Orthodox opinion, however, should not be depreciated. It is important what one believes concerning the great truths of the gospel. He tends to become what he believes. Orthodoxy of belief, however, is never an adequate substitute for consistent Christian living.

Certainly none of us fully and perfectly practices all Christ has commanded. We all fall short. We fail to express fully the spirit of Christ or to practice perfectly his principles. No wonder the verb form in the teaching portion of the Great Commission carries the idea of continuous action. We are to keep on teaching. We might be able to teach those who have been won to Christ to know what he taught; but if we are to lead them to practice what he has commanded, then our task is endless.

As we seek continuously to teach others, we ourselves need to continue to go to school to the Master Teacher. Let us hope and pray that we shall understand more fully what he

[8] Bruce, *op. cit.*, p. 340.

taught, shall see more clearly its application to race relations and to other problems, and that we shall be gripped by a deepening inner purpose to live in accordance with what we know.

"Lo, I Am with You Always"

The word "lo" or "see" or "behold" is found over sixty times in the Gospel of Matthew alone and almost as frequently in Luke. It was used by Jesus to introduce some great events and truths, but none more wonderful than these closing words of the Great Commission.

The "I" in the promise is emphatic. The "I am" is what is known as the prophetic present. Jesus did not say, "I will be with you" but, "I am with you." He spoke from the viewpoint of the eternal. In eternity there is no distinction between here and there, now and then. The "I am" reminds us of the words of God to Moses, when the latter wanted to know what reply he was to give the children of Israel when they asked him the name of the God who had sent him to deliver them. God's reply to Moses was, "Say this to the people of Israel, 'I Am has sent me to you'" (Ex. 3:14). God was and is the eternally present One. The resurrected and glorified Christ expressed something of this same idea to the aged John on the Isle of Patmos when he said, "Fear not, I am the first and the last, and the living one; I died, and behold I am alive for evermore, and I have the keys of Death and Hades" (Rev. 1:17–18).

How wonderful to have the promise of his presence! Who was this One who promised to be with his disciples? He was the risen and soon to be exalted Son of God. He was the One to whom all power had been given in heaven and on earth. His promise is to us as well as to those who heard him speak the words that day. He has promised to be with us "all the days" (Williams) or "always, day by day" (Weymouth), and "He has never broken any promise spoken." He will be with us in days of sunshine and in days of darkness, in "days of strength and of weakness, days of success and of failure, of joy and of sorrow, of youth and of age, days of life and day of death—all the days." [9]

He promises to be with us "down to the very close of the age" (Williams). His triumphant return at the end of the present age is implied here. "This blessed hope is not designed as a sedative to an inactive mind and complacent conscience, but an incentive to the fullest endeavor to press on to the farthest limits of the world that all the nations may know Christ and the power of his Risen Life." [10]

The promise of his presence, along with the hope for his return, should impel us to take seriously his Commission to make disciples of all nations, to baptize those won, and to teach them to obey all he had commanded. The promise of his presence, as is true of most promises of God, is conditional. He has promised to be with us if we will go in his name to carry out his Commission. We have no right to expect his abiding presence unless we are obedient to him.

On the other hand, it is glorious to know that his presence goes with his own as they carry his gospel to the ends of the earth. But we believe that his presence will just as definitely go with those who are social, moral, and spiritual pioneers for him. Christians generally tend to honor, and rightly so, those who represent them and Christ on foreign mission fields, particularly those who open new geographic frontiers. In contrast, many Christian people tend to ostracize those who seek to open up frontiers for Christ in our midst. And there are still many moral and spiritual frontiers, at home as well as on distant mission fields, that need to be entered and taken for Christ. Some of these frontiers are in the area of race.

One had better not attempt to enter these frontiers, however, unless he has a clear conviction that the Holy Spirit is leading him in that direction. He is not likely to follow the

[9] Broadus, *op. cit.*, p. 597.
[10] Robertson, *op. cit.*, I, 246.

path of the social and moral pioneer very far unless he has a deep sense of the presence of the resurrected Christ. The sense of the presence of Christ can and will give to the child of God the peace that passes understanding and the courage to carry on for Christ in the face of criticism and opposition.

Still another blessing that comes as a result of his presence, which helps to explain the quiet dignity and strength of God's pioneering messengers, is the assurance of ultimate triumph. The One who is with them is all powerful. He can know no ultimate defeat. There will come a time when the kingdom of the world will "become the kingdom of our Lord and of his Christ, and he shall reign for ever and ever" (Rev. 11:15).

As we examine our lives in the light of the Great Commission and all that it implies, do we have any justifiable ground for claiming the continuing presence of the Lord? Are we going, and as we go are we making disciples and enlisting them in our churches? But more applicable to our immediate concern, are we teaching those won and enlisted all the things Christ commanded? What is even more searching, are we applying those truths to our own lives?

What about the specific area of race? How consistently are we applying the spirit and the teachings of Jesus to our personal relations with those of other races and classes? Can we justifiably expect his abiding presence? We cannot unless we are doing our best in what we are persuaded he wants us to do, regardless of the circumstances surrounding us.

Conclusion

In response to the Commission of Christ our churches send missionaries around the world. We give our money to support them. We challenge the best of our young men and women to respond to the needs of a world without Christ. Many of the people among whom our missionaries work are colored. Most of those who do not work with colored people serve in areas where there is comparatively little race consciousness and discrimination. Peoples of all races are welcomed into practically all churches on mission fields.

The racial attitudes of individual Christians and churches at home frequently handicap those missionaries in their work. Any failure to be Christian in relation to other races here at home adds burdens to the backs of our representatives around the world. These failures are like chains around their legs and handcuffs on their wrists. Any injustice or discrimination based on race or color in our country is shouted from the housetops in other areas of the world. What is said in North Carolina today is known in Nigeria tomorrow! What happens in a small town in Tennessee or Texas literally is blazoned in the headlines of the papers of Latin America!

It becomes increasingly clear that the Christian forces of the United States have a "rendezvous with destiny." It seems that the future of the Christian movement in America and around the world will be determined to a considerable degree by what American Christians, both individuals and groups, do in the days immediately ahead about the racial situation in our midst. If Christians do not attempt honestly to apply the Christian spirit and Christian principles to race relations, how can they expect others to respect their Christian claims or to hear and accept the message they proclaim? The race problem is, in a very real sense, "American Christianity's test case."

VII

"THE POWERS THAT BE"

*Let every soul be subject unto the higher powers.
For there is no power but of God: the powers that
be are ordained of God.* ROMANS 13:1, AV

A careful study of Romans 13:1–7 may reveal that
what Paul wrote then is relevant to our day. We may find
the principles enunciated by him will provide some guidance for us as we face the perplexing problems created for
us and the world by the new racial situation. We also may
conclude that these verses, written by the Christian apostle
to a church group living in Rome in the days of Nero, were
and are "the corner-stone of civil order." [1]

Exhortation to Obedience

Notice, first of all, that the exhortation is universal: "Let
every soul" ("every person," RSV; "everybody," Williams;
"everyone," Goodspeed) be subject to the powers that be.
Weymouth very specifically individualizes the responsibility. He translates it, "Let every individual," while Robertson [2] suggests that "every soul" is a Hebraism for "every
man." The universalizing of the exhortation implies that it
involves a natural obligation. It is not a strictly Christian
requirement. This means that the obligation to obey rests on
Christians and non-Christians alike.

It is possible, however, that Paul made the exhortation to
obedience all-inclusive for the sake of some Christians in
the Roman community who thought that their loyalty to

[1] Handley C. G. Moule, *The Epistle of St. Paul to the Romans* (*The
Expositor's Bible,* ed. W. Robertson Nicoll [Grand Rapids: Wm. B. Eerdmans Publishing Co., 1940]), V, 603.
[2] *Op. cit.,* IV, 407.

Christ released them from obedience to the powers that be. Some of them may have developed a spirit closely akin to the Jews, who "were everywhere restive under Roman rule" [3] and "were notoriously bad subjects." [4] It could be that Paul wanted these verses, which are different from anything found elsewhere in his epistles, to counteract such an attitude or tendency. The verses are unique, so it does seem that there must have been some particular need for Paul's saying what he did. He plainly says that government as such is ordained of God and that every person should recognize and submit to its authority.

Jesus similarly counseled obedience to the powers that be, at least by implication, when he said, "Render therefore to Caesar the things that are Caesar's, and to God the things that are God's" (Matt. 22:21). The immediate thing that Jesus taught was that his questioner and the other Jews should pay their taxes. However, more than taxes belong to Caesar, and whatever belongs to him is to be rendered to him.

The conclusion, based on the teachings of Jesus and Paul, is that Christians should be law abiding and should be defenders of law and order. They should pay "taxes to whom taxes are due, revenue to whom revenue is due, respect to whom respect is due, honor to whom honor is due" (Rom. 13:7). This does not mean that the Christian should give respect only to the respectable or honor only to the honorable. The "due," or the debt, would depend upon the position held rather than upon the individual who held it. Peter also says, "Honor all men. Love the brotherhood. Fear God. Honor the emperor" (1 Peter 2:17). Governmental authorities should be honored and respected, even by those who do not agree with what they do. They should be honored

[3] Arnold and Ford, op. cit., p. 272.

[4] James Denney, St. Paul's Epistle to the Romans (The Expositor's Greek Testament [Grand Rapids: Wm. B. Eerdmans Publishing Co., n.d.]), II, 695.

and respected for the office they hold even if they are unworthy personally.

A number of years ago an army officer taught a raw recruit a lesson he has not forgotten. The officer was explaining the meaning and significance of the salute. In substance he said, "When you salute an officer, you do not salute that particular officer. You salute the uniform and what that uniform stands for." He further explained that the officer might be unworthy of the salute, but the uniform and the insignia on that uniform were due the respect implied by the salute. During the present controversy over the race issue, many people, including some Christians, have lost the proper respect for those in authority.

There is at least one other obligation, as revealed in the Bible, that rests on every Christian citizen. Christians should pray for those in authority. To Timothy, his "true child in the faith," Paul wrote as follows: "First of all, then, I urge that supplications, prayers, intercessions, and thanksgivings be made for all men, for kings and all who are in high positions" (1 Tim. 2:1–2). He then gives the reason for this admonition: "That we may lead a quiet and peaceable life, godly and respectful in every way." He concludes as follows: "This is good, and it is acceptable in the sight of God our Savior." Both the praying for kings and those in authority and the quiet and peaceable life that results from the praying are acceptable unto God. They are pleasing unto him because he "desires all men to be saved and to come to the knowledge of the truth." If Paul would exhort the Christians of that day to pray for and to be obedient to those in authority, how much more would he counsel those of us who live in a democracy to do fully as much.

Reasons for Obedience

There are many reasons why the children of God should be subject to the powers that be. In Romans 13 Paul clearly sets out several reasons for obedience.

First, there should be obedience because of the source of the powers that be and hence the source for the authority they have. They and their authority come from God. "There is no power but of God: the powers that be are ordained of God." Here the absolute sovereignty of God is implied. He is supreme over every authority. "All legitimate authority is derived from God's Authority, and the existing authority is appointed under God" (Phillips). This means that "the existing authority," whatever its form or nature, is responsible unto God. This is intimated by the statement Jesus made to Pilate: "You would have no power over me unless it had been given you from above" (John 19:11). At least God's permissive will was operative, or Pilate could not have had the authority or the power to put Jesus to death.

If the powers that be are ordained by, or derived from, God—and they are—then "he who resists the authorities resists what God has appointed" ("what God has established," Williams). Paul further says that "those who resist will incur judgment." Here is another argument for obedience. The Christian should be subject to the powers that be because God's judgment or wrath will come upon him if he is not. The judgment of God may be administered by those in authority, but in the final analysis it is his wrath or judgment. The word translated "wrath" in verse 4, when used in the New Testament, usually refers to the wrath of God. "It occurs eleven times in Romans," [5] always referring to the wrath of God.

Paul gives still another reason for obedience. In verse 5 he says, "Therefore one must be subject, not only to avoid God's wrath but also for the sake of conscience" ("as a matter of principle," Goodspeed). Subjection to governmental authorities must be "not only as a prudent policy, but also as a religious duty." [6] Thus we see that there is both an external (the wrath of God) and an internal (for the sake of

[5] Denney, *ibid.*, p. 697.
[6] Arnold and Ford, *op. cit.*, p. 274.

conscience, or principle) reason for obedience. Even if there was no fear of the wrath or judgment of God or the rulers, the child of God should recognize the divine source of the authority exercised by the government and submit to it.

Peter gives what might be considered another reason for obedience to the powers that be. He advises, "Be subject for the Lord's sake to every human institution, whether it be to the emperor as supreme, or to governors as sent by him to punish those who do wrong and to praise those who do right" (1 Peter 2:13–14). The submission is "for the Lord's sake." Doubtless "the Lord" refers to Jesus, as is practically always true in the writings of both Paul and Peter.

What did Peter mean when he used the expression "for the Lord's sake"? It might be retrospective, looking back to that which Jesus had taught and to the example he had set. It could refer specifically to his statement, "Render unto Caesar the things that are Caesar's." On the other hand, the expression might be prospective, looking forward to the effects of such conduct on the work of the Lord. If the latter viewpoint is correct, then Peter was saying, "Do these things for the sake of the Lord's cause." The context suggests that the latter is the correct interpretation of the phrase.

The people to whom Peter was writing seemed to have been under considerable suspicion and possibly were suffering some persecution. He suggests that they should be submissive to the emperor and to his representatives, that thereby they might "put to silence ("muzzle" or "gag") the ignorance of foolish men." Evidently these "foolish men" had brought charges against the Christians, and there is considerable possibility that those charges were that they were disloyal to the government. In the light of those charges, Peter recommends that they should be subject for the sake of the Lord's cause.

It is even possible that some of the Christians were tending to assert unduly, and to misinterpret, the freedom that they had in Christ. Some of them may have been, as is frequently true of Christians, "contentiously conscientious." [7] They may have thought that the experience they had had which made them new creations in Christ Jesus, with the resultant loyalty to him that this experience demanded, freed them from ordinary citizenship responsibilities. Whether this suggestion is right or not, it is interesting to notice that in the midst of this discussion Peter says, "Live as free men, yet without using your freedom as a pretext for evil; but live as servants of God" ("but live like slaves of God," Williams) (1 Peter 2:16).

Do you see the relevance of all of this to the contemporary situation? Every branch of our government—the legislative, the judicial, and the executive—belongs to the powers that be. They should be respected and not ridiculed. This should be true, even for those who may disagree with decisions made and actions taken.

Limitations of Obedience

Paul's expression "for the sake of conscience" and Peter's phrase "for the Lord's sake" might imply some limitations of the obedience or subjection. If one's primary concern is the Lord's cause, he might on occasion have to refuse to obey the commands of the state. If he obeys the authority for the Lord's sake, he cannot obey it when to do so would be contrary to the will of the Lord. As Wordsworth says, "Whenever *man* commands us to do anything that *God* forbids, or *forbids* us to do anything that God *commands*, we cannot and must not obey; for in such cases as these, in obeying man we should be disobeying God." [8]

The apostles recognized the limitations of any authority, civil or religious, over the conscience of the individual Christian. When Peter and John were charged by the rulers,

---

[7] Nathaniel Marshman Williams, *Commentary on the Epistles of Peter* (*An American Commentary on the New Testament*, ed. Alvah Hovey [Philadelphia: American Baptist Publication Society, 1888]), VI, 31.

[8] Arnold and Ford, *op. cit.*, p. 274.

elders, and scribes "not to speak or teach at all in the name of Jesus," they gave the classic answer to all such usurpation of divine authority. Their statement was: "Whether it is right in the sight of God to listen to you rather than to God, you must judge; for we cannot but speak of what we have seen and heard" (Acts 4:19–20). Later the high priest reprimanded the apostles, saying, "We strictly charged you not to teach in this name, yet here you have filled Jerusalem with your teaching and you intend to bring this man's blood upon us." The answer of Peter and the other apostles was, "We must obey God rather than men" (Acts 5:28–29).

Christians should not jump to the conclusion, however, that on the basis of these statements by the apostles they would be justified in disobeying their government. It seems, so far as the specific teachings of the New Testament and the example of Peter, John, Paul, and others are concerned, that there is only one defensible reason for refusing to obey constituted authority. The New Testament clearly reveals that no human institution has a right to deny to the child of God the privilege of proclaiming the gospel, of witnessing to its saving power. There may be other areas where the enlightened Christian conscience would dictate nonconformity, but Christians should be certain that there is biblical authority for such action.

When a Christian for any reason feels led to disobey the commands of the state, he should be prepared and willing to pay the price of his disobedience. It may be his privilege to suffer patiently the punishment of the state. He cannot in good conscience, however, seek to undermine or to overthrow the government, unless it would be "to obey God rather than men."

Christianity, when rightly interpreted, "lifts man to a sublime independence of his surroundings, by joining him direct to God in Christ, by making him the Friend of God." [9] It is this awareness of the presence of the Lord that has en-

[9] Moule, *Romans* in *The Expositor's Bible*, p. 350.

abled Christian men and women through the centuries to face calmly the opposition and persecution of the state and sometimes the church. Devotion to a higher loyalty has given courage to men "to stand upright in solitary protest for truth." It was this that enabled Luther to say, "Here I stand, I can do no otherwise. God help me. Amen." [10] The martyrs and the spiritual pioneers of the past have suffered willingly for their convictions. The climactic victories for freedom have been and "are won by those who 'endure grief, suffering wrongfully,' while they witness for right and Christ before their oppressors." [11] It was Peter who said, "If when you do right and suffer for it you take it patiently, you have God's approval" (1 Peter 2:20).

Conclusions Concerning Obedience

Think through and evaluate the following brief summary of the teachings of the New Testament, particularly Romans 13:1–7, concerning the state and the Christian's relation to it.

1. The state or government as such is of divine origin.

2. There is nothing explicit in the New Testament that would justify, at least directly, any revolutionary action that would attempt to overthrow constituted authority. This does not necessarily mean that political revolutions are never justified. It does mean that they cannot be supported by specific scriptural authority.

3. The general emphasis of the Scriptures, and of Romans 13, is on the duties of Christians rather than on their rights or privileges. The Christian is to be concerned primarily about the rights of others rather than with his own rights. He is to surrender his rights and privileges voluntarily, if necessary, for the sake of others and for the sake of the cause of Christ. This principle applies to his citizenship responsibilities, but it also has a wider application.

[10] Julius Köstlin, *Life of Luther* (New York: Charles Scribner's Sons, 1920), p. 240.
[11] Moule, *Romans* in *The Expositor's Bible*, p. 353.

4. Paul not only says that government as such is ordained of God and that Christians should be obedient to the powers that be, but he also says that those powers exist to approve the good and to disapprove, restrain, or punish the evil. This then is God's plan and purpose for the powers that be. The implication is that any government that fails to fulfil God's purposes will be under the judgment of God. In other words, there is a twofold obligation—on the citizen, but also on the government.

5. Where the demands of the government are contrary to the will of God, then the Christian is to obey God rather than men. God has reserved for himself the final authoritative word for the human spirit. When the Christian, in obedience to the inner voice of the divine Spirit, must disobey his government, he should do so with quietness and dignity. He should recognize not only his right of disobedience but also the government's right, under certain conditions, to punish him for disobedience. When such punishment comes, he should prove the depth of his conviction by his willingness to suffer for what he interprets to be the will of God. In other words, from the viewpoint of the Scriptures, martyrdom under certain conditions would be approved, while revolution by the use of force would not be. The cause of Christ has been advanced in marvelous ways at times by those who have been willing to die for him. In contrast, little Christian advance has been made by those who have been willing to fight for Christ. The word of Jesus to those who would fight for him was, "Put your sword back into its place" (Matt. 26:52). His kingdom, which is spiritual, cannot be defended, promoted, or advanced by the use of physical force.

6. While the precepts in the Scriptures in general, and of Romans 13:1–7 in particular, may have applied in a special way to New Testament days, they are abidingly applicable. Some of them are remarkably relevant to the contemporary period.

VIII

"CURSED BE CANAAN"

He said, "Cursed be Canaan; a slave of slaves shall he be to his brothers."   Genesis 9:25

The curse of Canaan, frequently erroneously referred to as "the curse of Ham," was used in the past to justify slavery. It is being used by some people today to defend the *status quo* in race relations. They interpret the curse to mean that the Negro, as a descendant of Ham, is destined by God to fill permanently a subservient place in society, that he should never be considered as an equal by the white man. On the basis of the curse, some even contend that the Negro is innately inferior and that he can never lift himself or be lifted to the intellectual, cultural, or even moral level of other races.

Background for the Curse

It may help us to interpret the curse of Canaan more accurately and to apply it more consistently if we will examine the background for the curse. If we are to understand this background, we must begin with Adam and Eve and study the cumulative effects of sin on the human family.

The record of the temptation and fall of Adam and Eve reveals that the consequences of sin are social as well as spiritual. Eve first surrendered to the wiles of Satan, but her sin did not stop with herself. Adam responded to her suggestion and partook of the forbidden fruit. No man or woman sins unto himself or herself. Other people are involved directly or indirectly, sooner or later, in and by one's sin.

The garden experience also reveals that sin separates men

from God. Sin caused the first couple to hide themselves from God. The record says that God sent Adam "forth from the garden of Eden" (Gen. 3:23). In a very real sense, however, it was sin that drove Adam and Eve out of the garden and from the presence of God. After committing sin, they no longer could remain in his holy presence. Sin separates us from God, or God separates us from sin.

Sin is also divisive in human relations. It tends to separate men from their loved ones and from their fellows. This result of sin is seen with particular clarity in the experience of Cain. After he killed his brother, not only was he driven from the place where God had manifested himself and hence in a sense from the presence of God, but he also was separated from his family. He became a fugitive and a wanderer on the face of the earth.

The way God handled the Cain-Abel experience may contain some suggestions for human relations in general and for race relations in particular. The questions that were asked by God and the one asked by Cain are interesting and quite significant. God's first question to Cain after he had killed his brother was, "Where is Abel your brother?" (Gen. 4:9). This has been one of God's most persistent and searching questions through the centuries.

Cain lied and replied, "I do not know." He then asked God a question that man has continued to ask: "Am I my brother's keeper?" (Gen. 4:9). God in turn asked Cain another question which continually searches the heart and haunts the soul of man. God's question was, "What have you done?" (Gen. 4:10). The questions God asked Cain he would ask you and me today. They have tremendous implications for race relations. "Where is our brother of other races?" "What have we done to him?" We cannot escape our responsibility for him by saying that we are not our brother's keeper. God answered that matter not only for Cain but for every man who has lived since the days of Cain.

106

What was God's answer to Cain's question? He did not give Cain a categorical yes or no, but we know by the way he handled the situation that his answer was, "Yes, you are your brother's keeper." That is his answer to any man and every man. We are our brother's keeper, and "brother" is not to be restricted to one who is our blood brother or even our spiritual brother in Christ. We are responsible unto God for our fellow human beings. They are our human brothers, members of one human family, although they may not be our brothers in the fullest spiritual sense.

There is at least one other thing in the Cain-Abel story that may have some significance for race relations. Some of the advocates of the contemporary racial pattern emphasize considerably the fact that "the Lord put a mark on Cain." A few even contend that Cain was turned black, that this was the mark placed upon him. It is of interest to know that the Hebrew word translated "mark" is found approximately eighty times in the Old Testament and here is the only place where it is translated "mark." It is translated "ensign" twice, "miracle" twice, "token" fourteen times, and "sign" over sixty times.[1] Many commentators suggest that the mark was a secret or an inner sign given to Cain to assure him that he would not be killed. For example, Dods says, "It is difficult to conceive of any visible mark which should warn men not to touch Cain, and a mark which should merely identify him would of course be rather a danger than a benefit."[2]

Whether the correct translation in this particular instance is "mark" or "sign," its purpose is clear. It was protective rather than punitive. Even assuming that it was a physical mark, easily identifiable by men when they saw Cain, it was

[1] See George V. Wigram, *The Englishman's Hebrew and Chaldee Concordance of the Old Testament* (London: Walton and Maberly, 1866), I, 33–34.
[2] Marcus Dods, *The Book of Genesis* (Edinburgh: T. & T. Clark, n.d.), p. 24.

to warn them that any one who slew Cain would have the vengeance of God fall upon him.

The cumulative effect and the deepening shadow of sin is revealed further in Genesis 6. There it says that the sons of God took wives of the daughters of men. There are several more or less common interpretations of the "sons of God" and "daughters of men" in the passage. The leading viewpoints are: (1) The sons of God were men of rank, position, and power, and the daughters of men were from the lower classes. (2) The sons of God were angels, who had physical relations with the daughters of men. (3) The sons of God were from among those who worshiped the true God. It is possible that they were descendants of Seth, while the daughters of men were from among the Cainites, who worshiped false gods. (4) Somewhat the reverse of the preceding, the sons of God referred to the men of Cain. The term had no spiritual connotation but merely referred to those who were physically strong or mighty. The daughters of men would refer to the daughters of Seth.

Without examining each of these in detail, which would require more space than justified, let us assume that the reference is to the marriage of the descendants of Seth to the descendants of Cain. Was God's displeasure based on the racial or the religious nature of the intermarriage? It seems definitely to have been the latter. "The evil here described is that of promiscuous intermarriage, without regard to spiritual character. The godly took them wives of all; that is, of the ungodly as well as the godly families, without any discrimination." [3]

Regardless of the viewpoint concerning Genesis 6, it seems clear that God's main concern, at least in this case, was with purity of worship rather than with purity of race. He was anxious and even jealous that his people worship him and him only. Actually, the intermarriage of Sethites

[3] J. G. Murphy, *A Critical and Exegetical Commentary on the Book of Genesis* (Andover: Warren F. Draper, 1866), pp. 178–79.

and Cainites from the racial viewpoint would be somewhat comparable to the marriage of Germans and English, but not of Caucasians and Negroes.

Whatever may be the correct interpretation of the "sons of God . . . daughters of men" passage, wickedness so multiplied in the earth that "it repented the Lord," or "the Lord was sorry" (Gen. 6:6), that he ever had made man. What does it mean when it says that God repented or was sorry? Repentance with man is a changing of the will; with God it is the willing of a change. God said, "I will blot out man," or wipe him off of the face of the earth. God chose the Flood to accomplish this purpose, although in his bountiful grace he delayed the Flood for 120 years to give the people a chance to repent under the preaching of Noah. This they refused to do.

Noah himself was a just or "righteous man" (Gen. 6:9), the first so designated, and he found favor in the eyes of the Lord. He and his family alone were preserved. His three sons were Shem, Ham, and Japheth.

After the Flood Noah planted a vineyard, made some wine, drank too much, and got drunk. While drunk he became uncovered, or literally uncovered himself. One of his sons, Ham, saw his nakedness and reported it to the other sons, possibly ridiculing his father or making immodest statements concerning him. When Noah awoke from his stupor, he found out about the incident and pronounced a curse upon Canaan, the youngest son of Ham.

Nature of the Curse

The first thing about the curse found in Genesis 9:25 is the fact that it was upon Canaan and not upon Ham. Why should Canaan, one of the four sons of Ham, be singled out by Noah? Why was the curse not pronounced on Ham, who was the offender? Were the other sons of Ham and their descendants included in the curse? There is no way to be absolutely sure about the answers to these questions. Some have suggested that God did not curse Ham because he had preserved him in the ark; to curse him would be inconsistent. Others suggest that he did not curse Ham because to do so would have meant that the curse would have been passed on to all the sons of Ham, and this was not God's purpose. There is another important question that we must come back to later: Was the curse from God or merely from Noah?

There are several possible explanations for the fact that Canaan rather than Ham was the object of the curse. (1) Ham was the youngest son, although incidentally this is not certain;[4] he would be punished through Canaan, his youngest son. (2) Canaan was involved in the sin of Ham and was possibly the real culprit in the crime. (3) Canaan already was walking in the sensual footsteps of his father, and Noah, having knowledge of this fact, used the occasion to pronounce judgment upon him. (4) The word "Canaan" here did not refer exclusively to an individual but was used in a collective sense to refer to the descendants of Canaan.

The last appears to be the best explanation for the curse of Canaan. Noah's words were prophetic. He foresaw the future character and destiny of Canaan's descendants and "made the act of Ham the occasion of the prediction which he uttered concerning them."[5] Noah's prophecy began to be fulfilled in the days of Joshua, "when the Canaanites were partly exterminated and partly reduced to the lowest form of slavery by the Israelites, who belonged to the family of Shem (Josh. 9:23; comp. Judg. 1:28); and it was subsequently fulfilled when those that remained of the Canaanites were reduced by Solomon (1 Kings 9:20, 21)."[6] Still later the de-

---

[4] See John Peter Lange, "Genesis," *Commentary on the Holy Scriptures,* ed. Phillip Schaaf (Grand Rapids: Zondervan Publishing House, 1949–51), p. 337. He says that the expression translated "his youngest son" (v. 24) literally means "his son, the little or the less." In the naming of the sons, Ham is in the middle (7:13; 10:1), as is also true of the listing of the descendants of the three sons of Noah in chapter 10.

[5] Goodspeed and Welton, *op. cit.,* p. 97.

[6] *Ibid.*

scendants of Canaan became the servants of Japheth when Carthage, "which had been settled by Canaanites, was conquered by Rome." [7]

There may not be enough evidence to be dogmatic about the reason the curse was pronounced on Canaan rather than on Ham, but those who cite "the curse of Ham" to justify the legal segregation of the races should remember that the record does not reveal any curse of Ham. Furthermore, there is no specific indication that the curse extended, or ever was intended to extend, to the other children of Ham. The other sons of Ham, as listed in Genesis 10:6, were Cush (Ethiopia), Mizraim (Egypt), and Phut (Put).

Those who emphasize the curse of Ham need to remember that some of the descendants of Ham, even some of the children of Canaan, were quite successful and prosperous. They built great cities, such as Nineveh and Babylon. They "were rearing palaces, digging canals, organising governments, and founding empires at a time when the descendants of Japheth were wandering over Europe with no better weapons than implements of flint and bone." [8] The Egyptians of the Hamitic line certainly built a great civilization. For several centuries the Israelites, descendants of Shem, served them. The psalmist refers to Egypt as the land of Ham (Psalms 78:51; 105:23, 26–27; 106:21–22). Incidentally, although the Egyptians are dark-skinned, they hardly could be called black.

The name "Canaan" meant "the submissive one," or "the depressed or low one." As suggested previously, it could be prophetic of the condition of the Canaanites in the future. The name itself stipulated that Canaan was to be a servant of servants, or a slave of slaves, to his brethren. It came to refer, however, to a place—to the land of Canaan. It first was used to refer to the low coastal areas of the eastern end

---

[7] Pieters, op. cit., p. 127.

[8] R. Payne Smith, Genesis in A Bible Commentary for English Readers, ed. Ellicott, I, 46.

of the Mediterranean but later was expanded to the Jordan valley and then to all the general area of Palestine.

It is generally agreed that the Canaanites, descendants of Canaan, were not black. In the main, they moved into Asia Minor and at least as far east as the Tigris and Euphrates valley. Other descendants of Ham went south into Africa, but not the Canaanites, upon whom the curse was at least specifically pronounced. Ryle suggests that "the application of this clause to the African races is an error of interpretation." [9] Similarly, Marcus Dods concludes, "Canaan being thus selected, the fulfilment of the curse must not be looked for in the other descendants of Ham, and still less in the negro races." [10] Pieters likewise says that "even if the Negroes be conceded to be the sons of Ham, they are certainly not descendants of Canaan, and these only are under the curse." [11]

Another interesting thing about the curse is its wording. Notice that it says, "A slave of slaves shall he be to his brothers." "Slave of slaves" is a Hebraism, a Hebrew method of expressing the superlative. It means that he is to be "the most conspicuous and lowest of servants" or "the most abject of slaves." [12] Similar expressions of the superlative found in the Bible are "vanity of vanities," "Holy of holies," "God of gods," "Lord of lords," and "King of kings."

Questions Regarding the Curse

Before we ask any question dealing specifically with the curse proper, let us jump ahead and raise a question about the tower of Babel. Was it connected in any way with the curse pronounced on Canaan? A reading of the record (Gen. 11:1–9) will reveal the reason for, and the purposes of, the confusion of tongues. Men determined to build a city, a

[9] Ryle, *The Book of Genesis, op. cit.,* p. 128.
[10] *Op. cit.,* p. 44.
[11] *Op. cit.,* p. 127.
[12] Smith, *op. cit.,* p. 46.

walled-in place, and "a tower with its top in the heavens" and said, "Let us make a name for ourselves, lest we be scattered abroad upon the face of the whole earth." God confounded their language. They then were scattered abroad, as possibly God had purposed from the first. We know that he had commanded the first couple to "be fruitful and multiply, and fill the earth and subdue it" (Gen. 1:28). It seems that men had failed to fulfil this purpose of God.

The record of the Babel incident also reveals that the children of men failed to recognize their need for God. They were asserting their independence of him. All that the experience at the tower of Babel (meaning "confusion") purports to explain is the presence of different languages in the world. There is not the least hint that it is supposed to account for the different races or is related in the least to the curse of Canaan.

Now, at some risk of repetition, let us consider a few questions concerning the curse of Canaan.

Was the curse from Noah or from God?

If we depend exclusively on the words of the curse, it was from Noah. God is not indicated as its source. Noah fails to claim divine authority. It is true that he used the name of the Lord in blessing Shem and Japheth. The fact that God's authority for the curse is not claimed is not conclusive evidence that God was not the real source of the curse. Assuming that the curse was prophetic, its later fulfilment would be rather substantial evidence that God was speaking through Noah.

Another rather persistent question is: Assuming that the curse was from God, was it upon all the descendants of Ham or only upon the descendants of Canaan?

We have already tried, at least to a degree, to answer this question. On the basis of the record we must conclude that the curse was pronounced only upon Canaan. Not a word is said about Cush (Ethiopia), Mizraim (Egypt), or Phut (Put). Hughes says, "Both the testimony and the silence of scriptural records support the view that descendants of Canaan only are the object of the curse." [13] The Negro is not a descendant of Canaan. He may have come from the line of Cush, although some scholars claim he is not a Hamite at all.

Hughes concludes that "since the terms of the curse were fulfilled with regard to descendants of Canaan only, the Negro is not included within the compass of the curse, and the curse has no relation to the color of the Negro's skin." [14] Some have assumed that the Negro got his color from his father, Ham, since the latter could mean "dark" or "black." However, Ham could also mean "warm" or "hot." If so, it could refer to the warm or hot climate where the Hamites lived. If it meant "black" or "dark," it could refer to the black soil in the Nile valley, where so many of the children of Ham settled. "It is unnecessary to conclude that the meaning of Ham's name refers to the color of any of his descendants or that it suggests that the curse includes all people who have black skin." [15]

Still another searching, but a rather hypothetical, question is: Even if the curse were meant for all the children of Ham —which is the only conceivable way the Negro could be included in the curse—are Negroes the only ones on whom the curse now rests? What about the modern descendants of the other sons of Ham—are they under the curse?

In the contemporary period the curse is being applied exclusively to the Negro. Why is this true? It seems at times that it is used as a convenient tool to justify wrong attitudes toward, and unjust treatment of, Negroes by many white people. When it is so used, it becomes a part of what the psychologists call "rationalization." Some members of the dominant white group want to justify their conduct. To do so they make use of Noah's curse and suggest that God himself has ordained that the Negro should fill a place of secondary

[13] Robert Lane Hughes, "A Critical Study of the Meaning of ארור in Genesis 9:18–27," unpublished doctoral dissertation, New Orleans Baptist Theological Seminary, 1956, p. 82.

[14] *Ibid.*, p. 98.

[15] *Ibid.*, p. 94.

status. Some even go so far as to say that God has made the Negro inferior and that he never is to be accepted as an equal in the society of men.

Here is still another question: Even if we could conclude that the curse applied to all the children of Ham, would it be perpetual?

There were many people in slave days who claimed that the Negro, as a descendant of Ham, was to be held in perpetual slavery. They claimed that God had so ordained it and that man had no right to change the purposes of God. Today many of the extreme defenders of the segregation pattern are saying almost the same thing. Some of them claim that the Negro's second-grade citizenship is the result of the curse and that men should not interfere with what God has ordained.

In contrast, others suggest that God's judgments against the sins of fathers are visited only unto the third and fourth generations. They contend that for God to continue for thousands of years the curse upon any man or the descendants of that man would be contrary to the spirit of the God we find revealed in the Bible, particularly as seen in the life and teachings of Jesus, who came to reveal the nature, the character, and the will of God.

Murphy, in his commentary on Genesis, says: "It is proper to observe . . . that this prediction does not affirm an absolute perpetuity in the doom of Ham or Kenaan. It only delineates their relative condition until the whole race is again brought within the scope of prophecy." [16] Similarly, Hughes concludes that the curse of Canaan "should be classified as a terminated curse." [17] One reason it has been terminated is the fact that, strictly speaking, there are no Canaanites today. Furthermore, Hughes suggests that theoretically the curse need never to have been operative in the lives of the descendants of Canaan. Jehovah did not permit the terms of

[16] *Op. cit.*, pp. 211–12.
[17] *Op. cit.*, p. 106.

the curse "to come into force until the development of the sin made necessary the application of the penalty specified in the terms of the curse." [18] In other words, God's curses as well as his blessings are conditional.

Possibly some concluding questions relating to the contemporary scene should be asked: Is there a possibility that many people have misinterpreted God's relation to, and his movement among, the races of men? May it be that he is on the side of the underprivileged in the present struggle? May men, even in the name of the Lord, fight against the purposes of God in our day?

These are questions that at least should make all of us stop and think. Any who are resisting God's movement among men can be sure that they will be defeated. His over-all purposes will be achieved. He will be triumphant. These are revolutionary days. There is movement and change everywhere. Judging the present by the past, we can be sure that God is creatively active in our day. Let us hope and pray that he will give us enough insight to know the direction in which he is moving and sufficient courage and grace to catch step with him as he walks in our midst.

Conclusions Concerning the Curse

What can we conclude concerning the curse of Canaan and its relevance to the contemporary racial situation? Some personal conclusions are as follows:

1. The curse was a pronouncement of a particular sentence on a particular sin.

2. The curse was a prophecy. Its main purpose was to predict the subjugation of the Canaanites by the children of Israel.

3. The fulfilment of the terms of the curse and the time of the fulfilment were dependent on the decisions and the conduct of the ones mentioned in the curse.

4. The curse of Canaan has no direct relevance to the con-

[18] *Ibid.*, p. 105.

temporary racial situation. The Negro was not included in the original curse, since he was not and is not a descendant of Canaan. Even if he were a descendant of Canaan, the curse itself is no longer in force.

5. Most men seek divine sanction for what they do or want to do.

6. In seeking divine sanction for enforced racial segregation, some have used the curse of Canaan, which they usually label "the curse of Ham," and the Bible in general to support their position.

7. Even Christians may defend racial segregation as the best method of temporarily and immediately handling a perplexing problem without doing great damage to the cause of Christ, so long as they will not use the curse of Canaan and other biblical incidents and teachings to support their position, and so long as they do not defend segregation as being the full and final expression of the divine will in human relations. When the latter is done, irreparable harm is done to the Christian movement and to the Christian witness at home and abroad.

Surely the God who created man in his own image, who made of one all men, who is no respecter of persons, who loved all men enough to give his Son for their salvation, and who taught us to love our neighbor as ourselves did not and does not intend that any man or any segment of mankind should be kept in permanent subserviency or should be treated as innately inferior, as second-class citizens in a first-class society.